Outreach Matters

Seventeen Principles for
Successful Missions

Outreach Matters: Seventeen Principles for Successful Missions

Scripture quotations, unless otherwise indicated, are taken from the Holy Bible, New International Version®, NIV. Copyright ©1973, 1978, 1984, 2011 by Biblica, Inc.™ Used by permission of Zondervan. All rights reserved worldwide. www.zondervan.com The "NIV" and "New International Version" are trademarks registered in the United States Patent and Trademark Office by Biblica, Inc.™

Scripture quotations taken from the New American Standard Bible® (NASB), Copyright © 1960, 1962, 1963, 1968, 1971, 1972, 1973,1975, 1977, 1995 by The Lockman Foundation. Used by permission. www.Lockman.org

Copyright ©2016 by Jonathan Nowlen
ISBN: 978-0-692-78922-3
All rights reserved. No part of this book may be reproduced in any form without permission in writing from the author, except in the case of brief quotations embodied in critical articles or reviews.

Printed in the United States of America.

Jonathan Nowlen

OUTREACH
Matters

17 Principles for Successful Missions

Jonathan Nowlen was raised "on the field." His parents were early overseas mission training center builders and he has spent a large portion of his adult life in cross-cultural settings all over the world. The richness and variety of his life experiences coupled with his unique ability to communicate those experiences make this an exciting and unique read.

Jonathan is a master storyteller. His stories are told in a way that will allow the reader to draw instant application points for making good decisions about short term outreach/mission trips. We can all learn a lot from other people's experiences, especially when the person sharing those experiences has the spiritual maturity to help us apply scriptural insight to the stories.

This book is loaded with spiritual epiphanies that the Holy Spirit can use to plant Christ-like character seeds in the reader's life that then can be watered and fertilized by your own life experiences "on the field."

If you love spiritual adventure, you are going to love this book. It will help prepare you to grab hold of the life that is "life indeed" and inspire you on your journey with the one who is calling each of us to join Him in reconciling people from every tribe, tongue and nation to Himself.

May His Kingdom come and His will be done on earth as it is in Heaven.

Jim Hall
Co-Directional Leader
New Heights Church
Fayetteville, Arkansas

Contents

Forward ix
Preface xi
Introduction xiii
Why Does This Outreach Matter? xv
CHAPTER 1 Becoming God's Go-To Person 1
CHAPTER 2 Live Ready — Don't Get Ready 11
CHAPTER 3 The Last Christian 'Right' 19
CHAPTER 4 The Twinkie Principle 29
CHAPTER 5 Making the Most of it 37
CHAPTER 6 You Get Out What You Put In 45
CHAPTER 7 Success is to Serve 51
CHAPTER 8 Stay Usable 59
CHAPTER 9 The Pursuit of Romance 69
CHAPTER 10 The Alien Mind 75
CHAPTER 11 You Smell 83
CHAPTER 12 The Arrow of Offense 91
CHAPTER 13 Survive or Thrive 99
CHAPTER 14 The Circle of Trust 107
CHAPTER 15 Stay Covered 111
CHAPTER 16 The Lay of the Land 123
CHAPTER 17 When in the Wilderness 135
Conclusion 143

Forward

I am very glad Jonathan has finally written this book. Years ago, he presented a lecture on short-term outreach to a team of our students who were about to leave for the other side of the world. "Lecture" sounds like a boring monologue, but Jonathan's talk was practical, entertaining, hilarious, and challenging. The stories were exciting, and the principles were powerful. Ever since then, I have shamelessly plagiarized from Jonathan's talk whenever I've taught on short-term missions.

Having pioneered a long-term missions project in a restricted access Muslim nation, I know that using short-term teams effectively in that kind of setting is not easy. The ministry Jonathan leads is using groups of young people to accomplish strategic, long-term transformation through short-term involvement. That's impressive!

Jonathan Nowlen is the perfect person to write this book. He knows short-term outreach like few others, and he really believes in short-term missions. He has been doing it himself for many years, and he's seen the good, the bad, and the ugly. He knows the pitfalls, and he's seen miraculous results.

He knows how to position young people for success, and prepare them in advance for the challenges they will inevitably face.

Nathan Andrews
YWAM *Mendocino Coast*

Preface

GOD WANTS YOU TO BE A HERO. He wants you to become heroes of the faith and champions of the Kingdom. A true hero is someone who has aligned his or her identity, character and potential into a targeted purpose. Many people choose not to live heroically, but I believe that as part of God's original design your life matters. God has created an environment in which your identity, character and potential are positioned to shape history as you discover your purpose. God doesn't require you to shine, but he designed you with the potential to blind the eyes of the enemy with the focused reflection of His nature.

How do you become truly heroic in the Kingdom of God? The biblical story of King David's three Mighty Men is a great example of the way that heroes operate. The third mighty man, Shammah, is my favorite, but there is an often overlooked part of that story.

"Next to him was Shammah son of Agee the Hararite. When the Philistines banded together at a place where there was a field full of lentils, Israel's troops fled from them. But Shammah took his stand in the middle of the field. He defended it and struck the Philistines down, and the Lord brought about a great victory." (2 Sam 23:11-12)

To any observer or military strategist it may seem understandable that when faced with being overrun by their enemy, the Israelite army decided *not* to die while defending a field of lentils. Think, "dying for a bowl of split pea soup!"

I believe the way to become like King David's three mighty men requires a different way of thinking. Many people can dig deep and rise to the occasion when a worthwhile opportunity knocks. We see this evidenced in every sphere of society and throughout history. This is generally how wars are won and great works accomplished.

A hero in the Kingdom of God, is a believer who rises to the occasion, but also rises when there is no occasion. Shammah is known throughout biblical history as a hero because he rose when there was really no occasion. He rose to defend a field of beans because he knew to whom those beans belonged. He valued the beans because he valued the owner. Heroes of the Kingdom choose to view average daily activity to be just as important and purposeful as the exceptional occasion.

We value the Kingdom because we value the King. If we are going to become heroes of the faith, we must focus on our inherent purpose and not just rise to an occasion. We must shine when there seems to be no occasion. No bean field should be relinquished to the enemy if we have anything to say about it.

I pray that this book inspires you to find your purpose and live heroically even if it sometimes appears that you are living and dying for a field of beans. The Kingdom is designed to need true heroes and contrary to many opinions, you absolutely matter!

Introduction

I'VE PARTICIPATED IN AND WITNESSED AN AMAZING 35 years of the expansion of God's kingdom on the planet. My journey started when I was four years old. Our family joined the missionary effort to win the world to Jesus. It has been an intense and sometimes arduous journey, yet one filled with awe inspiring experiences, often while walking an unknown path with Christ.

My first outreach away from family took place when I was 14 years old. My youth outreach team spent eight weeks witnessing about life in Christ and sharing God's story through the performing arts. We preached in Salt Lake City, Utah, in the Philippines and in China. Since that initial outreach, I have worked in more than 60 countries and have led or participated in more than 150 outreach efforts of various lengths, shapes, sizes and focuses.

In writing this book I want to turn those life lessons into an uncomplicated study. The goal of this study is to place in the hands of the next generation of Christian workers, the experiences, lessons and ideas that will maximize their potential to impact the world for Christ.

One key idea often reiterated in leadership training circles is the concept of "Failing Forward." This idea says, "It's okay to make mistakes, just make new ones." It is my hope that the experiences, lessons and ideas contained in this book will enable the next wave of youthful disciples to avoid making the same mistakes my teams made. I want you to build on our life lessons as you effectively reveal the Kingdom of God in your generation.

If the stories of our hardships, failures, successes and risks can be used to empower and champion those young people who are now expanding the Kingdom of God, it will be well worth all past sacrifices.

The principles and illustrations contained in this book are derived from my Kingdom efforts around the world. All of the life lessons that I illustrate have come from a rewarding life full of adventure and the presence of God. God does not rob us. He is not a God who demands and takes from us, leaving us empty and used up.

Our God is a God who desires to participate in and lead us through every moment of life. Through the hardships and the victories, and beyond, as the family of God seeks to fulfill His, "Great Commission," (Matthew 28:18-20).

It is my prayer that the principles contained in this book will help others go, "Further Up and Further In." One of my favorite authors, C.S. Lewis, articulates allegorically in "The Chronicles of Narnia" the idea of not settling for where your are, but instead pressing onward in the 'upward call of God in Christ Jesus." (Phil 3:14, ESV)

"I have come home at last! This is my real country! I belong here. This is the land I have been looking for all my life, though I never knew it till now ... Come further up, come further in!" (C.S. Lewis, *The Last Battle*)

As I've taught these principles around the world, to both new and experienced followers of Christ, I have often heard the same feedback repeated. It often sounds something like, "Why didn't we get this teaching *before* we undertook our Kingdom efforts?" Former students have also told me, "everything you taught us about successful outreach actually happened!"

However, whether or not these principles and life lessons are useful to you or helpful in your particular undertaking, I am glad, at least, that by reading this book you will have received a foundation and a head start that many in my generation never had.

Why Does This Outreach Matter?

YOU MAY NOT BE ASKING THIS QUESTION now, but when you are in the middle of some desolate, oppressed area of the world the question may come to dwell in the forefront of your mind!

I began asking myself a question like this, something along the lines of, "Why does this outreach matter, and why am I here at all?" I was arranging my sleeping mat in a canvas shelter erected on the high plains of the Himalayas. The icy wind was tearing through me, ripping every bit of warmth out of my body. Ice was beginning to form on my soaking wet boots and clothing. My hands, and my mind, were so numb that it was nearly impossible to retrieve and position the 40-pound rocks onto the edges of our tent. These rocks were necessary. They were the only way to prevent our tents from being blown away by the 50 mph winds. At this point in our 75-mile trek, at over 14 thousand feet, I would have given almost anything to be rescued by helicopter. I would also have taken rescue by donkey, yak or by any other means available if I had my way!

But there was no rescue and no easy way out of the extremely difficult situation we were in. The small canvas shelter had no closable door. Just an end open to the elements. We had to set up our sleeping mats on soaking wet grass that had sheep droppings covering every square inch of it. The temperature dropped below five degrees Fahrenheit at night and soared to over 80 degrees in the daytime. During the first three days of the trekking phase of the expedition the altitude was robbing me of so much oxygen that I was unable to retain short-term memory.

We were hiking 12 miles per day at altitudes up to 16 thousand feet. The only way I was able to recall what happened each day was by looking back at the pages of the journal that I had dutifully filled out over the course of the previous days. We were in bad shape.

I had come to the Himalayas to meet up with this particular team directly from mild and balmy India, and my body had no preparation and no chance to acclimatize to the high altitude and the wildly different weather. This trek was the first part of the mission we knew God wanted us to undertake during our month long expedition. God wanted to establish His kingdom in this desolate place, but since the time of Noah there had been almost no gospel progress here. Now, for one of the first times in over five thousand years, there was a real opportunity to bring the Gospel into this region. We were determined to allow the Lord to lead us into very dark places.

The word of the Lord was clear, the access had been granted, the season of openness in political and spiritual history was obvious. Now, all that remained was to persevere and obey. First our team set out to research the spiritual history of this recently opened region. Then we were to explore deep into the territory. We were bringing the good news of redemption through Christ's sacrifice. This was a confrontation to the stronghold of the kingdom of darkness that had always covered this desolate, isolated area of the world.

Once there, we quickly discovered that the devil was not about to let us enter his house and rob his possessions without offering some serious opposition. As we crossed raging glacial rivers on the backs of feisty yaks, it was easy to understand why this part of the world was unreached, and why no one had yet succeeded in planting a long-term, transformational faith community in this region. Our team's common refrain during this expedition was 'all the easy places are already reached'.

The first night of our trek we set up a base camp. Our five-day, 75-mile trek would launch from this remote, roadside location on the following morning and we needed to get some sleep. My tent-mate, Jeremiah, was a friend from back in the USA and he was excited to be on this trip. We spent the first two hours hauling rocks to hold down our canvas tent and then spread some plastic sheeting over the tent to keep out the cold rains and melting snow that oppressed us.

We huddled in our sleeping bags and tried to stay warm, but it soon became apparent that the devil was well aware that we were in his territory. I had finally begun to doze off when I was awakened by a loud series of grunts and exclamations, and saw my friend partially out of his sleeping bag, flailing wildly around the tent. Jeremiah was in a full-blown wrestling match with an unseen but very real entity that was attempting to overpower him.

I was so tired and so cold that I had no sense of fear as I observed this wrestling match through the small breathing vent I had left open in my mummy bag. More than anything, I was annoyed. Tomorrow we had a 12-mile hike and I really wanted to sleep! "You need help?" I loudly whispered to Jeremiah. "No, no, I've got this," was his reply as he grappled with an invisible demonic spirit. I had experienced many supernatural encounters in my life prior to this, so while I was skeptical that he was not in need of assistance, it was obvious that as he struggled and prayed with authority that he was confident.

All I could think to say as I turned over and drifted off to sleep was, "wake me up if you need help,"... then I turned over in my sleeping bag and went to sleep. About an hour later I was awakened to Jeremiah punching me through my sleeping bag and saying, "Ok, ok, I need some help!"... So I sat up and prayed with him against the attacking spirit and it immediately left him alone. I had just started to doze off once again, and Jeremiah began to catch his breath, but the afflicting spirit was back. This cycle of spiritual conflict went on most of the night, with Jeremiah waking me twice for assistance. By about 4:00 AM, he had prayed and struggled through the attack and the spirit left for good.

When the 6 AM wake-up call was sounded we began packing our camp. We were dead tired, but incredibly pumped up with faith and confidence in the power of God. We had overcome a major spiritual attack by the power of the name of Jesus. We had needed this faith-building experience far more than we had needed a solid night of sleep!

Near the middle of the trekking portion of this outreach, most of our team had strongly considered any options we could think of for abandoning the cause. We had run out of food, hiked through a blizzard, had been challenged by a sorcerer who was following us up the mountainside, forded waist deep raging glacial rivers, carried our exhausted team members on yaks, survived 80 degree temperature swings, and were reduced to drinking water from parasite-infected streams. I think we all would have given up and bailed out if we'd had the option.

There was much discussion of sending for helicopter rescue, buying a yak herd to ride on, or even of sending for help from a distant city. The problem with these desperate ideas was that none of them were in any way possible! There simply was no way to survive other than to finish the trek and reach our vehicles at the end of the route. By God's mercy and grace we survived this trek in the Himalayan wilderness. Imagine, this was only the first six days of a five-week expedition!

Days after the trekking phase was finished, we drove into a small, but beautiful town on the main road. Although we had the appropriate permits and permission to be in this area of the Himalayas, the local officials in the town could not and would not believe that it was possible that we had permission to be there. They immediately confined us to our small hotel, essentially putting us under house arrest. Leaving our rooms was not allowed. We even had to request escort to the one, tiny shower facility available to us. Things were not looking positive or productive for this phase of our trip.

A young police officer who was put in charge of watching our group became our, "man of peace," (Luke 10:6) in the city. This officer had a very compassionate heart particularly for the many orphans in the area. He had setup a small orphanage which he funded using much of his meager government salary. After we befriended this young officer he negotiated a way to take us on a walking tour of the city. As we walked the city and followed our new friend he proceeded to show us the most significant locations.

We stopped at one particularly large Buddhist monastery. Our police officer guide was not willing to attempt to enter the temple. Instead he waited outside as we were welcomed in by one of the lead monks. As we made our way past hundreds of very bemused monks, we entered the inner chamber or main meeting hall where their worship rituals were carried out. In this place, massive, four-foot-wide drums were being thunderously pounded as dozens of monks sitting in rows, rocked back and forth in the dim candlelight. The goal of this vociferous and reverberating ceremony was to summon a demon god to the temple.

The architecture of the hall was the vibrantly painted and ornate structure, embossed with gold, which is typical of monasteries in this region. The yak butter candles that had burned perpetually for thousands of years created so much smoke and haze that it actually became hard to breathe. The cloying smell of these hundreds of candles made my stomach gather in knots. The odor seemed to repel any sense of the presence of the One True Lord. The spiritual darkness in this monastery was unchallenged and unimaginable to the average Christian sitting at home.

We walked past the staring eyes of the carved demon gods that lined the walls of the temple, and ended up standing in front of a colossal, ten-foot, castle-style, wooden door. We now had a middle-aged, Buddhist monk as a tour guide and he proudly pointed to the giant door we were facing. One member of our group spoke the local dialect. The tour guide monk asked if we wanted to see the sacred treasure room. Of course we did. Excitedly he hurried off to find the key for the lock that was obviously an ancient mechanism. Nearly an hour later the monk returned with the key. He explained that it had been almost 50 years since anyone opened this particular vault door and it had taken a lengthy search to locate the giant key. He further explained that he had found the key on a necklace around the neck of an elderly monk who was at that moment on his deathbed.

Our tour guide monk was excited and really antsy at the same time as he opened the massive door. No one on our team could have imagined what was inside. Our initial expectations for the "treasure room" were very constrained. The door opened to reveal a 15-foot tall, gold-plated Buddha sitting at the center of a 30 foot by 20 foot room. The room was filled with haze, and dust hung in the air. As the light filtered in from the temple we began to focus our eyes on piles and piles of gleaming treasure. There were 16 solid-gold Buddhas that about twelve inches tall. Each one sat on a pedestal. They were arranged all around the base of the massive, gold-plated Buddha. On shelves, and piled on the floor, were gold, ancient weapons and other precious items.

The sight was hard to focus on and my eyes didn't know what to look at first. We stared quietly as we tried to understand what we had just stumbled into. The monk proceeded to point out that we were the first people who were not a part of that monastery, to ever see this treasure. He also explained that all this treasure had been deposited here by the desperately poor local population over the course of the last few thousand years.

Truly curious, we asked the monk about the history of this place. The monk explained that in this form of Buddhism, this kind of impoverishing sacrifice would ensure a better reincarnation. The massive pile of treasure represented the desperate measures and brutal lengths that the people would consent to, in order to find forgiveness for their sins. What a travesty and a grievous deception the devil had orchestrated against these people. People God had created, and for whom Jesus died!

People in every culture are usually aware, to some degree, of their own sin and feel a need to pay a penalty for their guilt. All people have a deep need for their consciences to be cleansed. These are the kinds of desperate and tragic developments that arise when people worship false gods and try, in their own strength, to acquire forgiveness, immortality and peace.

Your outreach matters! These scenarios of deception, destruction, and the ensuing hopelessness will never be changed until these lost and dying souls realize that the way of salvation has already been purchased! You bring the message of liberation - the message that their hope for salvation and immortality has already been made possible through the price that Christ paid. They can keep their gold and treasure. God only wants their hearts. This is the good news! This is the reason you are involved in these outreaches and Kingdom efforts. *"How beautiful on the mountains are the feet of those who bring good news, who proclaim peace, who bring good tidings, who proclaim salvation, who say to Zion, 'Your God reigns!'"* (Isaiah 52:7).

Did you know that God intends to win this historical contest for the hearts and souls of men? You and I have the privilege and responsibility of being part of the fulfillment of the 'Lord's Prayer'. Jesus prayed, "Your Will be done on Earth as it is in Heaven." We live in an incredible era of spiritual history. Right now, more people convert to Christ every 30 minutes than converted to Christ on the day of Pentecost!

The Old Testament prophet Zephaniah declared that, *"The Lord will be awesome to them when He destroys all the gods of the land, the nations on every shore will worship Him, everyone in their own land."* (Zeph 2:11) The New Testament enlarges this thought in 1st Corinthians 15:24, *"Then the end will come, when He hands over the kingdom to God the Father, after He has destroyed all dominion, authority and power."*

As servants of our victorious Lord and Savior, we are on the winning side of spiritual history. We have to keep this in mind as we move forward in taking spiritual ground from the, "ruler of this world" (2 Cor 4:4), the devil. We must strive to understand and maintain Jesus' perspective. God wins.

God is more excited than you are about your efforts in His Kingdom! You are working in close cooperation and agreement with the very heart and nature of the Lord. He does not want anyone to perish. We have the privilege of working to accomplish the highest plans of the Lord for all the people of his creation. You have the highest level of approval and support for your effort in the Kingdom. God himself is your greatest fan and supporter. So do not be intimidated, do not be discouraged, the Lord will change the world through you!

Chapter 1
Becoming God's Go-To Person

I AWOKE TO A KNOCK ON THE door of my tiny, World War Two-era room. It was early —really early— far too early for anyone to be disturbing me on the first day off I'd had during this three-month field assignment in Ukraine. We were there in response to an unprecedented season of spiritual hunger and openness that had followed the recent collapse of communism in the Soviet Union. At the six-week mark, our outreach had already been an adventure-filled success. Often up to 1,000 people were becoming Christians each day in response to our witness of Christ, and hundreds had been miraculously healed!

And now we were tired. Incredibly tired. On most days we had presented three evangelistic events, walking as much as six miles between event locations, while hauling our equipment by hand. Our team of 14 was staying in the top floor of a four-story building that had been built as refugee housing in 1946. It was a rough place, but we found some sense of security and comfort in the fact that we had the whole floor of the building to ourselves. Accommodations had been rough on this outreach. For example, our housing did not have showers, so if we wanted to shower we had to hike down to the basement of the building to a place we affectionately referred to as, "The Shower Dungeon."

The shower dungeon was accessed through a medieval looking cellar door from the *outside* of the building. Stepping into the basement facility was an experience on the same level as voluntarily stepping into a B-grade horror movie scene. There was one light bulb that barely hung to the ceiling and dully cast an eerie light on inches deep standing water that filled the entire basement of the building. The shower heads were just taps that were tied into the water pipes in the ceiling overhead. In my imagination, entering the shower dungeon was like a movie where the foolish characters are promptly eaten by alligators while the movie audience screams unheeded counsel at the screen! Needless to say, no one on our team was devoured by creatures in the shower dungeon. However, *creepy* and *miserable* are good words to describe the shower experience in this building.

These are some of the reasons that when that 6:00 AM knock on my door came on my only day off in six weeks, I was not feeling ready for anything else. However, despite my feelings in the moment, I had become aware that God often asked me to do things that no one else would do. Obeying God and being accessible to Him always felt like a privilege and an honor, and so the one thing I strove to do was to hear and obey what the Lord was speaking to me at any given moment. Choosing a "Yes" response as my normal, day-to-day priority, had made me what I began to call, "God's Go-To Person."

What I mean is that when God wanted something done He could depend on me to hear, and at least *try* to obey. Through many years of walking with the Lord and attempting to honor all that I have believed He was asking of me, I have concluded that there could be no other truly meaningful way to live. The Bible says, "*The **secret of the Lord** is for those who fear Him, and He will make them know His covenant.*" (Ps 25:14)

I can think of nothing that compares to walking through life with the creator the universe whispering secrets to me as His friend. This is the heart attitude that a follower of Christ must pursue and value if wanting to become one of God's go-to people.

I stumbled out of bed and cracked open the door to find one of the young women from my team impatiently waiting outside. I could see immediately that she had been crying and was obviously upset. I peered out at her through the narrow space and before I could even say a word, she quickly and tearfully shared her situation.

Yesterday at our last open-air evangelism meeting, she had shared the gospel with, and prayed for, a 10 year-old girl. This young girl spoke fairly good English. I remembered the young girl, having briefly met her after the event. When this Ukrainian girl invited my teammate to visit her school on the following day, my teammate quickly agreed, not knowing that the next day would be an official, "team holiday."

We had a wise rule for our team: no girls were allowed to venture out without bringing one or more of the male team members along with them. It was extremely dangerous during those days for a young woman to be out by herself in this part of the world, so the rules were not without reason. Once my teammate realized that it would be a day off for the team, on the very day she had promised to visit the girl's school, she began imploring and negotiating with the guys on the team to go with her. One by one, each of the guys had made it clear to her that they were not interested in leaving their rooms on this, our one and only, day off.

She finally found my door with only minutes remaining before her window of opportunity to visit the school would be closed. She had begun to pound on my door, but without much hope that I would agree to go with her. As I blearily stared at her through the cracked-open door, I managed to get the idea of what she was asking me to do. Let's be clear: I did not want to go in the slightest! However, as she paused to catch her breath, I mumbled, "Give me a second," and I shut the door. Leaning my head against the door jam, I resolved to listen to the voice of the Lord and to do what He told me to do. Immediately, I heard the still small voice of the Lord say, "Go, I want to do something through this." I opened the door and said, "All right, I'll go."

I quickly dressed and we headed out the door at a fast walk. We had to navigate the eight-mile distance on foot, as there was little or no public transportation available in those days. As we approached this ominous, Soviet-style building, it became clear that the massive complex was alive with hundreds and hundreds of children and teenagers. It began to dawn on me that this was highly abnormal as it was mid-July and the Ukrainian school term had ended at least six weeks earlier. My teammate had no more idea why this school was full of noisy and excited young people than I did, and had not given it any thought.

We entered though a side door and, amazingly, the young girl who had invited us was watching for us at the appointed time. Once she located us she quickly took us into her classroom and we briefly met her teacher. Her teacher was in a hurry, and urgently directed us to share some stories with the class to help them work on their English comprehension. The only thing that came to mind was to share a few typical Sunday School-type Bible stories, such as, *Noah*, and *David and Goliath*. We were able to share the Gospel story for a short, three minutes, and then the class ended. After saying good-bye to our young student friend, the teacher and the other students, we began to wander the hallways toward the front of the building, looking for the exit. We still had no idea what was going on in this mysterious summer school facility.

As we searched for an exit, the thoughts pounding inside my head were not positive. I couldn't believe I had given up my free day to share about *Noah and the Ark* with a bunch of 10-year-old students. I struggled to keep my attitude in check as we walked though the building. Suddenly, out from a door on my right, a middle-aged American woman literally jumped in front of us and said, "You! Are you a Christian? We are teaching English using the Bible. I'm all the way to the Crucifixion, but the students are just not getting it, —so get in there and preach!!"

With that command, she grabbed my arm and shoved me through the door into the front of the classroom where I found myself staring at more than 100 college students! The students had a mix of various expressions on their faces. Many were uninterested, some were confused, and some were openly hostile to the message of the Gospel. They all stared back at me as I stared at them in a barely-veiled state of shock. I had never preached more than the basic gospel message in my life! These students had already heard the gospel at length, and if this opportunity was to not be wasted, I was really had to *preach*!

Then a miracle happened! As I began to fight off a wave of fear and intimidation that welled up inside of me, I suddenly found myself speaking. The Holy Spirit proceeded to take over, filling my mind with inspiration, and shaping the very words that were coming out of my mouth! This had never happened to me before!

Scripture says in Matthew 10:19-20, *"But when they hand you over, do not worry about how or what you are to say; for it will be given you in that hour what you are to say. For it is not you who speak, but it is the Spirit of your Father who speaks in you."*

This promise suddenly manifested its truthfulness in me before the eyes of not only this class, but also my stunned teammate! As I began speaking, words and insights that I had never thought about began to eloquently flow from my mouth. In the back of my mind I was saying to myself, "This stuff is amazing, I should write this down!"

I went on preaching for nearly an hour, speaking on the atonement, sacrifice, holiness, sin and a number of other key topics. After a brief pause at the one-hour mark I began to take questions from the students. Tough questions! But the answers that flowed out of me were deep and rich with insight and understanding. To this day, I don't really remember much that

I said. And still I thought, "This stuff is really good, I should write this down!"

There is a vital part of scripture that we do well to remember. 1 Corinthians 1:27 says *'but God has chosen the foolish things of the world to shame the wise, and God has chosen the weak things of the world to shame the things which are strong.'* Out of my obvious weakness and inadequacy, God had chosen to display His love and power to this group of students. I was as surprised as they were at what was being shared through me.

I could tell by their wide eyes and rapt attention that the students were held in enthused interest by what the Holy Spirit was saying. When the Q&A session ended, I suddenly found myself silently staring back at the students who stared at me in dead silence. Slowly, a girl toward the back of the class, who was obviously the class spokesperson, raised her hand and stood up to speak. She said, "We have never heard this message presented like this before. You must come back to this school tomorrow and share with all the students." "Sure," I said. After this Holy-Spirit-inspired oratory miracle, I was not lacking confidence.

As we slowly returned to our housing block I could not help but wonder what this would lead to the next day. Once we returned to our team and told them the story about my preaching miracle, and also about the invitation we had received from the student leaders to return on the following day to present the Gospel to *all* of the students, the rest of the team was extremely excited and ready to go for it!

Many times, all God is looking for is a willing and available vessel through which to show Himself powerful. It was obviously wasn't my amazing talent as a public speaker, nor my well studied, and carefully-constructed evangelistic message that made such an impact on those students. It was the Holy Spirit fulfilling his promise from Matthew 10:19-20, and in so doing, he was securing all the glory and all the praise for himself. For my part, I was extremely happy to attribute it all to him.

The next morning the whole team was up early and ready to go. Breakfast was a tortured affair, as were most meals in that city during those days. Even if you had money you could not find any location to actually purchase food. There were no restaurants in operation except for one bold pizza place. Unfortunately, we had learned to avoid the pizza restaurant after our first visit. We had exhausted an entire day searching on foot for this rumored location, and once we finally found it, we piled into its red, vinyl-cushioned booths. As we ecstatically began trying to figure out how to order pizza or any form of food that resembled pizza, we began to notice that our booth was riddled with bullet holes. Apparently, the owner explained to us, on the previous day, there had been a mafia hit in the restaurant and a number of gangsters had been killed in that very booth. Needless to say, after this we decided not to frequent this known haunt of the local mafia.

Back at our breakfast restaurant, we were served a famous Russian soup known as Borscht, which I really grew to love, along with the standard menu of coleslaw and dark brown bread. However, to call this place a "restaurant" is to be overly generous. It was a Soviet, "soup kitchen." A place where you could come and eat even if you had no money to pay. It was a dismal place to eat, but we made the best of it. At first we were traumatized by the cockroaches that floated to the surface of our soup, and the maggots that inundated our coleslaw. However, after a few days, and driven by hunger, we relented and began not only to eat the Borscht, but also to amuse ourselves with attempts to flick the cockroaches out of our own soup bowls and land them in the bowls of unsuspecting team members across the table! (They were boiled, and therefore harmless, we told ourselves.) So on this day, as on many others, after we had completed another adventurous borscht breakfast, we headed out on the long, urban trek to the school complex.

The day could not have gone better! We were welcomed by a group of student representatives and ushered into a huge, open hall, where 800 students were packed in and standing, waiting for us to arrive. Quickly, we set up for our performing arts program and went for it! After the performance we shared testimonies of the personal transformation we had experienced in our own journeys with God. Then our team leader and I were able to share the gospel message again, but this time with the entire student community. To my great surprise, more than 300 students passionately responded to the message of salvation and we were able to lead them into the Kingdom of God that very day!

These young people were able to hear the gospel and received a chance to respond to it because I was willing to give up my "day off" in obedience to the Lord. Living with the intention of being one of God's "go-to-people" is largely about whether you are willing and available. If you determine that you will prioritize listening to the Lord at every moment, keeping your mind set upon Him, He will choose you to work with Him on the things that matter to Him.

In my experience, the choice that holds back those who claim to want to serve God, (and have even made significant sacrifices to do so), is the idea that we can set up "boundaries" with God. We may not do this intentionally, but we find ourselves saying in the back of our minds things like, "I'll do this or that, as long as He doesn't send me Africa"... or something along those lines.

We begin to create subconscious walls that we feel will "protect" us from trespassing on the fringes of our comfort zones. You will never have the privilege of being God's, "go-to person" in the Kingdom if you allow these walls to remain. If He knows that you won't be willing, then He won't approach you to do the work, and you will not experience the reward. There really is a true reward to be found. Even if you fail in your attempt to radically obey, which everyone does at some point, you will find that you have brought pleasure to the heart of God, and that His eye is on you long after you have forgotten the events that you felt were such a failure.

You can position yourself for life-long favor from God by being willing to make the attempt. Unlike us, God doesn't judge a situation by the end result; instead, he is more concerned with your heart and motives during the journey. The means to the end are just as important to him as any perceived success or outcome that we envision as an acceptable end-result. The Lord can get us to our destination by many means and through many routes, but the process we go through to get there is where one's life story is truly written.

The walls or boundaries that we set up in our hearts and minds regarding our interaction with God are the same walls and boundaries that will define our future in the Kingdom. The reason these walls are so important is because their substance is created by our lack of understanding of the character and nature of God. The more tightly these false constructs cloister our spiritual life-flow, the more clearly evidenced it is that we do not understand or trust the character and nature of God.

Psalm 145:5-13 clearly portrays the character and nature of our Lord.

*"On the glorious splendor of Your **majesty**
And on Your **wonderful works**, I will meditate.
Men shall speak of the power of Your **awesome acts**,
And I will tell of Your **greatness**.*

*They shall eagerly utter the memory of Your abundant **goodness***
*And will shout joyfully of Your **righteousness**.*
*The Lord is **gracious** and **merciful**;*
*Slow to anger and great in **lovingkindness**.*
*The Lord is **good** to all,*
*And His **mercies** are over all His works.*
All Your works shall give thanks to You, O Lord,
And Your godly ones shall bless You.
*They shall speak of the **glory** of Your kingdom*
*And talk of Your **power**;*
To make known to the sons of men Your mighty acts
*And the glory of the **majesty** of Your kingdom.*
*Your kingdom is an **everlasting** kingdom,*
*And **Your dominion endures** throughout all generations."*
(emphasis mine)

Evidence that you are slandering the character and nature of God can be found in the following types of thoughts or statements;

- As long as He doesn't send me to '_____'
- As long as I don't have to do '_____'
- As long as I don't have to work with so and so.
- As long as someone pays me to do '_____'
- As long as my friends approve.
- As long as my family agrees.
- As long as this doesn't interfere with '_____'
- As long as this won't cost me anything.
- As long as I don't have to give up my day off…

Allowing these types of thoughts and beliefs to continue in your life defines you as a person who does not believe that God is who he says he is. This type of unbelief leads to a life of debilitating doubt, self-preservation, fear and self-centeredness. As children of God, we have to identify and resist any thoughts that set themselves against God.

> *"We are destroying speculations and every lofty thing raised up against the knowledge of God, and we are taking every thought captive to the obedience of Christ."*
> (2 Cor 10:5)

Becoming one of God's Go-To-People is not complicated. The source of such a life flows from a heart that is tightly knit to the heart of Christ.

Starting a new life as a follower of Christ is an exciting and rewarding time! We discover that life is about getting to know the Creator of all things, and that we are in the most amazing love relationship available to mankind.

As you open your heart completely to God and learn to let him prove himself to be who he claims to be, you will find yourself walking through life in the most amazing and fulfilling way imaginable. You will be blessed, and the Lord will be blessed as you trust him and trust his direction in your life.

Becoming God's, go-to-person is really about becoming trustworthy. The reason God allows tests and trials in your life is because He is testing your responses, choices and character. As you make right choices and repent for wrong ones, you show yourself to be increasingly trustworthy. Embrace testing and trials, because when you come through them successfully you will attract the attention of the Lord.

Romans 5:3-5a says *"And not only this, but we also exult in our tribulations, knowing that tribulation brings about perseverance; and perseverance, proven character; and proven character, hope; and hope does not disappoint..."*

If you leverage your tribulations and turn hard experiences into hope, you have truly come to know the ways of God and you will not be disappointed in your walk with God.

2 Chronicles 16:9a says, *"For the eyes of the Lord move to and fro throughout the earth that He may strongly support those whose heart is completely His..."*

If you want the *strong support* of the Lord in your life, then the scripture says you must have a heart that is completely His. This is the essence of becoming God's, go-to person. Being completely His requires you to live intentionally and position yourself for action in the purposes of God by 'Living Ready.'

Chapter 2

Live Ready — Don't Get Ready

MANY OF US HAVE A SENSE OF calling, a sense of destiny that resonates deeply in our souls. Sometimes this sense or awareness is stirred into action by what we see or hear, or by the things we experience in life. All people are gifted and called by God, but few of us actually see our callings and dreams realized. What makes the difference? What sets apart the people who seem to excel or reach a high level of effectiveness in advancing the kingdom of God, from those who do not?

I believe that *truly successful people are those who spend their lives to ensure that the dreams of God are realized on the planet. This is the definition of success that resonates for eternity.*

Young and old Christians alike often hear themselves praying like this; "Lord use me! I want to serve you!" Yet, often these same people never seem to be released into ministry or service to God. God is not willing that any people should perish. He is also in the business of using average people to accomplish transformation and reconciliation in this fallen world (see 1 Cor 1:27). So then, what distinguishes those who appear to make an impact with their lives in the service of Christ from those who feel they never realize their calling? I would suggest that some of the factors are in our own hands.

How do you position yourself for God to release you or activate you in your calling? You have to *Live Ready* because you will not have time to *Get Ready*. The Bible compares the Christian life to the life of a soldier with good reason (Eph 6:11-17, 2 Tim 2:3, 4). No soldier would wait until he had his deployment orders or assignment in hand to begin training and preparing. This would be a completely irresponsible and dangerous way to operate a military. Soldiers are educated constantly, train daily, and keep their weapons clean and ready; they embrace a focused and disciplined life. This is the key to effective readiness in military service, and these principles are not significantly different for people who seek active deployment in the service of the King of Kings.

Are you ready for deployment? One of the best ways to assess your level of readiness is to listen to your own prayers. Do you hear yourself saying things like, "Lord Use Me," or, "Send Me, Lord," yet find yourself sitting on the bench while others start in the game? You may even find yourself overseas, or in an outreach setting and, though the lost and needy are all around you, these same words are filling your prayers. You feel unused, on the outside, or like God is ignoring you.

In this section I am writing to those who are, "children of the burning heart," as A.W. Tozer calls those whose hearts burn in their deep awareness of and relationship with God. If your heart is positioned before God with a yearning to serve and bless Him with your obedience, and you are ready to accomplish what you feel He is asking you to do, you may deeply connect with this discussion. Once you have closely walked with God and the things that matter to him burn in your heart, you may understand the sense of frustration that comes when you feel that God has called you, only to then leave you on the bench, so to speak.

If this is you, I want to first assure you that God did not call you into His service only to park you on the bench. However, I have a tough-love message that may apply to you: If you constantly hear yourself praying, "God use me," it may be that you are not yet God's go-to-person. God's starting lineup is for everyone. Jesus said, "The harvest is plentiful but the workers are few." There are not enough workers to have any of them sitting on the bench. How then do you become usable in Christ's service? Let's look at some keys to the principle of becoming one of God's "go-to-people."

First, you have to become fully submitted to Him.

"For the eyes of the LORD move to and fro throughout the earth that He may strongly support those whose heart is completely His." (2 Chron 16:9)

Your personal relationship with God is the only thing that will propel and sustain you beyond a transient, emotionally compassionate response to the calling of God on your life. What must be cultivated is a deeply connected, burning passion for the lost that is an outflow of a true love relationship with Jesus. If your motivation is anything other than, "doing what I see my Father doing" (John 5:19), in loving and obedient agreement with the heart of God, you will falter. You must cultivate a heart that loves what God loves and hates what God hates.

Early in my walk with God, during my high school years, I began to intensely seek to know God in a real and personal way. I was desperate. I did not want to have just good behavior, or my own righteousness. God was very real to me but I wanted to really know Him as a *person*. At that time I began to cultivate this relationship with God by fasting from sleep. I told God that I was going to pursue Him forcefully until I was able to find Him and walk with Him. I began to read the Bible late at night for up to six hours per night. I was going through the Bible cover-to-cover every six weeks. I was intrigued that this was possible. The Bible speaks of Enoch, who, "... *walked with God: and he was not; for God took him.*" (Genesis 5:24). He was so close to God, such a friend of God, that he walked with God as a friend during his life on earth. The Bible says that then he "was no more." God took Enoch up from the earth to continue their relationship face-to-face. That is a relationship with God to be envied!

Through the work of Christ, all of us have the potential to walk with God in this same manner. Let your heart be completely His. As I pursued relationship with God with sincere intensity, I truly met God and I even began to have highly supernatural encounters such as visions and interaction with angels. My heart began to feel what God was feeling when I was in any environment or situation. The Holy Spirit began to compel me into my calling. Like a match coming into contact with a magnesium strip, the closer I came to the presence of God, the more my calling began to ignite. My potential and calling was activated.

Eventually I found myself, as a teenager, standing on a balcony in Odessa, Ukraine. Looking out over this massive city that had almost no known Christians, my heart began to grieve and burn for the lost. I remember stretching out my hands and speaking out words that must have come straight from God. I was asking Him questions, "What can be done," and, "What can *we* do?" God began to ask *me* what *I* thought of the situation. From that night onward, I knew that when God tested my heart He found that it was "completely His." Then He gave me great support (anointing), as promised in scripture, to literally change the destiny of nations through the work of the Gospel.

Avoid Entanglements

"No one serving as a soldier gets involved in civilian affairs—he wants to please his commanding officer." (2 Tim 2:4)

Living Ready requires that you limit your entanglement in "civilian affairs." In other words, you have to keep yourself free from the cares of the world. This doesn't mean that you must completely ignore the world or join a monastery or convent, but it does mean that you manage your life well. If you become entangled in the things of this world, even things that are not wrong, you risk being unable to "please your commanding officer." So stay free! Keep your priorities straight and your life focused.

What are some key areas that you must keep yourself from being entangled in? These are two of the most common that I have observed:

1 — **Distracting relationships.** The famous saying, "show me your friends and I'll show you your future," is very true. You become like those with whom you associate, so make very careful choices about those with whom you will spend time. Similarly, dating and romantic relationships have to be carefully considered. As a general rule I strongly recommend that you seek God to settle your calling with him before you settle your romantic pursuits, otherwise you might waste a lot of God's time chasing relationships that are incompatible with what he has in store for you.

If you are serious about pursuing your calling in ministry or missions, keep that as the primary filter in your mind and heart as you consider who you will allow to catch your romantic interest. If your proposed significant other does not have the same worldview and calling that you do, your calling and ministry could become handicapped. You will likely live a long and blessed life, but certain things that could have been may not end up being. Choose carefully.

2 — **Debt.** This seems logical and straightforward, but it is a serious concern. Many people forgo or delay their calling and service to the Lord due to the tyranny of debt. A few practical examples are college debt, car loans and credit card debt. These things are not inherently wrong, but they will entangle you. If you really want to position yourself for usefulness in missions or other ministry, keep yourself as free as possible. If God were to say "Go!" would you be able to get up and go? Ask yourself this question often and let the answer guide your actions and decisions.

Pursue Good Stewardship

As we position ourselves for service in missions or ministry, not only do we have to avoid certain things, but we also need to intentionally engage certain things. Positioning yourself to be free to respond to the call of God will require that you are very careful in how you steward the following areas of life. If you are to accomplish anything significant in life, it will require trade-offs. You will have to prioritize how you use your limited time, money, and talents.

1—Time. Each day you have opportunities to be intentional about how you will spend every minute. Although much of our daily time is consumed with obligations, for example, we are obligated to actions such as sleeping, eating, hygiene (hopefully), and work. The rest of our time is subject to discretionary use. This is the area that must be managed in a focused way if you are to position yourself for service in the Kingdom. If we misuse these resources that God has given us, not only will we not realize our calling and potential, but God will not be able to trust us (see Luke 16:10). I suggest that you view your discretionary time as raw material that can be shaped. If you choose, you can turn time into an effective weapon against the enemy of your soul. Each day you have opportunities to turn your spare time into a lifestyle of action that will continually develop your calling and potential.

2—Money. Just as with your time, you have a certain amount of money that you would consider discretionary. If you are using your spare money solely on entertainment, this may be an indication that you need to make some changes. Money gives you an opportunity to enhance your skills and potential; for example, instead of loading up on all of the most recent video games, you could purchase developmental resources. Instead of a going to a movie, you could save the money for ministry opportunities you know are coming. Be careful with your money because it really is God's. If you are a wise steward of the little money that God has trusted you with now, you will be a good steward of great resources in ministry. Luke 16:10 says, *"Whoever can be trusted with very little can also be trusted with much, and whoever is dishonest with very little will also be dishonest with much."* Spend your money on things that will help you advance the kingdom and 'Live Ready' to respond to the call of God.

3—Talent. As John Maxwell wisely stated, "Talent is never enough." All of us have many gifts and talents that God has built into us. These talents are custom designed by God to equip you to be a mechanism of blessing to the world. The challenge with talent is that it requires cultivation and development. Developing your talents is also an area of stewardship. Sometimes people have a sense of their basic gifts and talents, but their character weaknesses like laziness or selfishness, keep them from activating those gifts. While some people may neglect or misuse their talents, you have the opportunity to invest the time and energy necessary to develop your talents into something that can be used powerfully by God! Your talents and gifts, combined with the uniqueness of *you*, are a potential explosion of blessing to the planet when empowered by your relationship with God. If you steward your talents well, God will find in you a willing and available vessel that He can shine through in this dark world.

If there is one *Golden Key* to being released into ministry and service to God, I believe it is to live a developmental lifestyle! By, "developmental" I mean, live a lifestyle of growth. Follow the example of Christ! One often overlooked aspect of the life of Christ was his very normal upbringing, he grew and developed. He went through all of the phases, ages, temptations and trials that every young person goes through. Christ is the ultimate example of release into effective ministry. It is wise to consider his example if we desire to be effective in the kingdom.

—*—

"And Jesus grew in wisdom and stature, and in favor with God and man." (Luke 2:52)

There are several central ingredients to Living Ready, and this scripture contains some of the most important ideas.

The first big idea is that Jesus grew. Some growth happens naturally. You naturally grow upwards for a certain amount of time, and then you begin to grow outwards if you are not careful. But the scripture indicates that Jesus' growth culminated in, and was defined by, favor with God and man. Jesus grew in wisdom; we must be diligent to live the lifestyle of a learner. Study, read, learn and grow at all times, not just in school. I have often heard young Christians say "The last book I read was back in high school,"

"Back in college," or "Back in my missionary training program," etc. This person is *not* Living Ready.

However, be aware that it is also important to diversify your reading material. For example, I used to be an avid reader of novels. This was something I had truly enjoyed from the time I was in Junior High school. There came a time, though, when I realized that reading novels was taking up precious minutes and mental energy that could be focused into Living Ready, so I minimized my time reading novels and got focused.

A friend mentioned to me that he finds it hard to get into the books that he knows he should be reading. My response to him is, "We all need to be reading books that are a matter of life and death for others." In other words, the books you choose to read should inspire you with the idea that, "If I master this content it could save or change other people's lives." Reading books that matter becomes rewarding as you begin to find yourself better equipped and further sharpened in your ability to effectively serve in God's kingdom. Read the right stuff, with the right perspective. It is a key to Living Ready. If you are not reading, you will not find yourself leading, but if you are reading and studying, you will grow in wisdom. Learn from the lifestyle of Christ.

The second big idea is that Jesus grew in *Stature*. Apparently, his stature was such that the stewardship of his physical body was looked on favorably by God and Man. If you want to Live Ready, you have to be a good steward of your physical body.

One of the reasons that we have an unreached area of the world, almost two billion people, is that those people live in locations on the planet that are physically difficult to access. I learned a hard lesson about my lack of physical stewardship when I first traveled to the Himalayas. I had neglected my physical condition since high school. I ate whatever I wanted, I was physically inactive much of the time, and I had no idea that the outcome of these behaviors would be a serious limitation. I thought I was *ready* to go any place God called me. However, when I began to do some light physical training prior to outreach, I found that I was in dismal physical condition. When I later arrived in the Himalayas, I realized I was in trouble.

One day into that six-day, 75-mile trek, at altitudes often above 14,000 feet, I had the revelation that I had not been a good steward of my *stature*. While I may have survived that trek physically, most of the time I was not an asset to the team in any physical sense. I realized that in this kingdom calling, we usually don't have time to *get ready* for our calling… we have to Live Ready. This requires different priorities and intentional stewardship of time, treasure and talent. Because I had not Lived Ready, I had to then make some lifestyle changes. Fortunately, I was able to learn this valuable life lesson. Since arriving home from that trip, I have maintained a consistent emphasis on taking care of my physical body.

No soldier would get far in his mission if he waited until the night before deployment to start getting in shape; and his commanding officer would be foolish to send someone so ill prepared into the battle. The goal is not to pursue some idealized fixation on your personal physique, but that you would honor God with your body and grow in *stature* in a way that is pleasing and useful to God. My goal of staying in shape and taking care of my health was successful and sustainable because my motivation was to Live Ready for God and his service.

Do not be afraid of Discipline. Instead, embrace and value a disciplined lifestyle. None of the principles of Living Ready that I have mentioned so far are possible to achieve without living a disciplined life. In this context, we are not speaking of punishment when considering discipline, though the discipline that comes through punishment is not an entirely bad thing. The Bible is clear that God disciplines us because he loves us as his children. By 'discipline' I mean, "Training to act in accordance with rules; drill; activity, exercise, or a regimen that develops or improves a skill; training."

Train and master your rebellious flesh. You have to master it. Being disciplined in your lifestyle, being "Disciplined to Destiny," is the only way to make tangible progress in life. You only reach your destiny by embracing discipline.

I was motivated by a desire for God to activate me when He needed someone to do his work. If you take the things that matter to God seriously, you will make the trade-offs necessary to be able to stay off of the bench and start the game.

Live Ready, be a life-long learner, be a good steward of your time, treasure and talent, and you will find yourself at the top of God's roster of available ministers of His gospel and stewards of His kingdom.

Chapter 3
The Last Christian 'Right'

It was the, "Wild West" era in Russia's far Eastern region known as Siberia. Law and order were in short supply in this volatile and remote area of the world and, again, I found myself in the middle of an arduous adventure in this broken and hurting area of the world. Getting to the Siberian city of Krasnoyarsk had been an adventure all its own.

After three days and two nights' travel on a vintage, Soviet-era train, we had arrived in the remote city of Krasnoyarsk. I was traveling with another friend from the United States and we had begun our journey from Moscow to Siberia not really knowing what lay ahead on this assignment. This was my fourth such adventure in the former Soviet Union during the early and mid 1990's, but this time we were leaving the better-known western republics and the well-known western cities of Russia and heading to the edge of civilization in Siberia.

This area of the world is stunningly beautiful. If you fly from Moscow to Krasnoyarsk you experience an unending ocean of ancient forest that stretches from horizon to horizon for the entire four-hour flight! And this is only halfway across Siberia. Our train trip over the same distance seemed to go on forever without a break in the solid walls of trees that lined the railroad tracks. Occasionally we encountered remote railway stations built of dreary grey concrete, but even then the train rarely stopped. This was the "fast train" from Moscow.

Of the many events one could never anticipate on these train trips, one of the foremost was the kind of cabin-mate to be had. It was not unusual to discover what the wildest imagination could not have dreamed, and this trip proved to be no different.

We were in a train car compartment containing four bunks. My friend and I took the two top bunks. On one of the lower bunks, I could have sworn, was the current president (at the time), of the Russian Federation,

Boris Yeltsin. I did a full double-take when I entered the room. This guy could have been a body double! This gregarious character, who was a fan of Russian Vodka, immediately jumped to his feet and loudly asserted that I must be a professional boxer, while he solidly pounded on my chest with his small fists. He was excited to have Americans in the compartment with him, and especially one who he was certain he had seen in a professional boxing match in Moscow! He would not be convinced otherwise, so I went with his quirky assumption and quickly hit it off well with Boris Yeltsin's doppelgänger. As the train began to pull away from the station in Moscow, he proceeded to open a bottle of Vodka and extract piles of the most awful smelling dried fish you could ever imagine. Drink! Eat! He insisted.

In the time I had spent in the former Soviet Union, I had learned over the years to make friends with my train car cabin-mates if I wanted to arrive safely and with all of my belongings intact. I joined him for this traumatic dining experience. Boris didn't speak much English and I spoke only basic Russian, but his antics proved to be an amusing relief in the midst of an incredibly long and boring train ride. The trip turned into an endless experience of smelly dried fish, faked sips of vodka, and Boris demonstrating his boxing moves at every opportunity. As the days on the train slowly passed I began to feel God's heart burning with compassion and unconditional love for these people. I was excited to be able to participate with God in what was burning in His heart. Once again, our proverb, "There is never a dull day in Russia," proved true.

My assignment on this trip was to serve with a group of volunteers conducting discipleship camps for young, new believers. This was my third assignment with this particular project during the mid 1990's, and I was excited to join with old friends from previous adventures and welcome a new group of team members. We were committed to seeing the foundations of faith established in the lives of hundreds of young people who were becoming Christians during this incredible season of openness in Russia.

The team we joined in Krasnoyarsk was newly formed. The field team leader that we were working with was a young man named Jay. He had been in Russia for a number of years and had adapted well to the culture. He spoke Russian reasonably well and had even married a Russian woman from that region. This was going to be complex project, involving a number of small, new churches from the Krasnoyarsk region, and I was about to find out how difficult it could be to work with new churches who had not yet become disciples.

When we arrived in Krasnoyarsk, Jay picked us up at the station and we made our way across the city toward his apartment. Krasnoyarsk was much the same in appearance as most cities of Soviet design in that era. Endless rows of matching concrete apartment blocks, wide main streets and nondescript multi-use buildings. Cities in Russia that did not have the older historic buildings, from before the communist era, were incredibly bleak. One often had a strong sense that the soul of the people had been forcibly removed from their very existence. I found this even evident in their eyes.

During this era I found that I could invariably identify Russians in a photo or a group of people by the deadened appearance of their eyes. The old saying that, "the eyes are the windows of the soul" seemed to be very true in this case. However, given that their very identity and dignity had been crushed by the godless system of the former Soviet Union, it was not surprising that these people would have suffered such deadening in their souls. Now that they were free, so to speak, it became clear to me that people are not enslaved by any particular external system as much as they are enslaved by the condition of their own hearts. Freedom is the message of Christ: freedom from sin, shame, guilt and condemnation. True freedom is not regulated by what government system you live under but rather by who governs your heart.

> "It was for freedom that Christ set us free; therefore keep standing firm and do not be subject again to a yoke of slavery." (Gal 5:1)

Russians were now free in a social and political sense. However, they had not yet been set free in their hearts by Christ. Slavery of the heart and soul still governed their lives: even the new believers. Much like the Galatians to whom the Apostle Paul wrote, the young Russian converts we worked with had yet to daily walk in the freedom that was theirs in Christ Jesus.

We soon discovered that the real challenge of this assignment wasn't the conditions in Siberia, the bad food, or even the complex ministry environment. The real challenge was that Jay, the field leader, was not doing well. He was really struggling in his personal and family life. Jay was under constant, soft persecution from the Orthodox Church, the local KGB office, and a number of dysfunctional local Christian leaders and pastors.

Our assignment was to help him organize and successfully operate two large youth camps in a remote forest area. They were located approximately six hours' drive outside Krasnoyarsk. As one of his primary helpers for the summer, I witnessed his peculiar web of challenges first-hand.

Hundreds of middle school and high school students from a large number of local churches were scheduled to attend our camps. Not only was the logistical side of this project incredibly complicated, but to add spice to the whole mix, we discovered that none of the local churches were in right relationship with each other. Repairing the unity of the churches became one of our primary desires.

Our strategy looked something like this: These churches were sending their young people to our discipleship programs, where we taught on fundamental discipleship subjects such as forgiveness and repentance, and other tenets of the faith. We believed God for his healing and intervention. We were excited to see how God would begin healing relationships in the local body of Christ — beginning with their own young people — and we were optimistic that we would ultimately see dramatic changes in the condition of the local body of Christ.

Our first night in Jay's apartment was terrifying! It was a small, one-bedroom apartment, and we found ourselves floor-camping in the living room in our sleeping bags. Normally, I would have been fine with this scenario as I had slept on many different floors during my short missions career. Jay had even found carpet in Siberia and had the only carpeted floor in Krasnoyarsk! As proud as he was of this carpet we quickly realized why no one else in this region attempted to carpet their apartments.

I awoke with a strange feeling. Sleeping on the carpeted floor had seemed like a really good idea the previous evening but now something was really wrong. As I lay on my side staring out at the room I detected movement on a large scale. The street lights were casting a weird, lighted glow into the apartment through living room windows. In this light I saw the floor moving. It took a moment for the reality of the situation to dawn on me and I jumped to my feet. The carpet was literally rolling like small waves in a lake! I woke my friend and we quickly grabbed our sleeping bags and climbed onto the living room furniture.

Under the carpet, hundreds of cockroaches, the large kind, were crawling about the living room! They created such force that the carpet was moving in waves that were clearly visible. I'd seen a lot of hideous things in my previous travels and work oversees, but this situation was over the top. We remained carefully positioned on top of the small living room chairs and tried as best we could to go back to sleep. That was not easy. It took all of my focus to keep calm and not open my eyes. Graciously, by morning all the cockroaches had retreated back down the dingy air vent in the kitchen, and the carpet had ceased to be a rolling mass. It was fortunate that I only had to make it through a few more nights at this apartment.

Jay, our field leader in this project, faced many more difficulties than cockroaches. Not only was he going through a painful time in his family life, but he also received weekly visits from representatives of the Russian Orthodox Church. One day I happened to be at the apartment when these representatives arrived for their weekly visit. To Jay's credit, he let them in and offered them tea. Once everyone was seated in the living room, comfortably sipping tea, the representatives proceeded to helpfully explain to Jay that instead of working for the cause of Christ, he was actually working for the anti-Christ and was an agent of Satan. Jay listened politely and then, at the end of their monologues, he gently disagreed with their assertions. They became extremely frustrated and upset that Jay just couldn't see that they were correct in their assessments! Because this was a regular occurrence, these events greatly contributed to Jay's declining morale.

We are often quick to judge a person or a situation without really knowing what is going on, or why things are the way they are. I found myself beginning to doubt Jay's effectiveness as I observed his erratic behavior, personal struggles and questionable decisions. He seemed to be slow to make decisions in general. He was not able to see an obvious, correct direction presented straight to him. He was emotionally unstable due to the hardships in his personal life. Often when in a meeting with Jay, I could see what decision needed to be made, what words needed to be said, and in what manner. But Jay usually made the wrong decision or initially said things in the wrong way. Later he realized his errors and attempted to fix things as best he could, but it was usually not possible to clean up all of the consequences that had resulted.

I felt the Lord telling me to keep my mouth shut during this process. However, when many of the local church leaders and even other international volunteers began to openly oppose his leadership in the project, I wasn't surprised. We were still at least a week away from the start of the programs we had planned, but the whole enterprise was beginning to crumble, not entirely due to Jay's struggling leadership, but because of the rebellion toward him that was brewing among the Christian workers.

After one particularly dysfunctional meeting had led to open confrontation and verbal resistance toward Jay and his leadership choices, I knew things had come to a crisis point. Once the meeting was finished and all others had left his apartment, I was standing quietly, thinking about what I had just observed. I distinctly heard the Lord speak to my heart that I was to, "Support Jay in every way and in every decision." The Lord said, "I want to do something amazing through this situation and through Jay."

Just as I had comprehended what I heard the Lord speaking to me, Jay turned to me with tears of frustration and hurt in his eyes. He said, "Are you with me, Jonathan? Can I count on you?" Even though I felt at the time that I would have made different, possibly better, decisions, I chose to obey what I felt the Lord had spoken to me, and offered my support to Jay. As I communicated to him that I would back him up and support his decisions, I could see a strong sense of relief in his face as his whole countenance softened. Jay was grateful to know that he was not alone.

> *"I have been crucified with Christ and I no longer live, but Christ lives in me. The life I now live in the body, I live by faith in the Son of God, who loved me and gave himself for me."* (Gal 2:20)

As followers of Christ we call this, "Dying to Self." The life we now live, we live by faith in Jesus. Practically speaking, dying to self can be seen as giving up your *rights* in this life in order to gain the Kingdom of God. Laying down rights as a Christian is understood to be a natural part of being conformed to Christ. This is a list of some of the rights that we willingly seek to lay down, or release, when we have repented of our sins and have chosen to follow the Lord. This compilation from Scripture is loosely attributed to Elizabeth Elliot.

- The right to take revenge (Rom 12:19-20)
- The right to have a comfortable, secure home (Luke 9:57-58)
- The right to spend our money however we please (Matt 6:19-21)
- The right to hate an enemy (Matt 5:43-48)
- The right to live life by our own rules (John 14:23-24)
- The right to hold a grudge (Col 3:13)
- The right to fit into society (Rom 12:2, Gal 1:10)

- The right to do whatever feels good (Gal 5:16-17, 1 Pet 4:2)
- The right to complain (Phil 2:14)
- The right to put self first (Phil 2:3-4)
- The right to express one's sexuality in ways that are contrary to the ways of God (1 Cor 6:18-20)
- The right to rebel against authority (1 Pet 2:13-15)
- The right to sue another believer (1 Cor 6:1-8)
- The right to end a disappointing marriage (Matt 5:31-32)

In Krasnoyarsk I discovered that I needed to give up the, "Last Christian Right," this is what I call, "The Right to be Right." I knew that Jay was making many bad decisions with this project and that if I were in his position I would make very different choices, what I felt would be "right" choices. Now it is clear to me that the issue was more about me and my team members than about any questionable decisions Jay was making. The real question I felt God ask me shortly after my expression of support for Jay was, "Do you trust Me in Jay?"

Warning signs that you have not given up your *Right to be Right* or that you may be operating from a spirit of pride can include hearing yourself say things like:

- I know how this should be done.
- If I were in charge…
- This is the way to do this…
- I can't believe so and so said to do things like this…
- I'll just go along with it.
- It's not my fault if this doesn't work.

Did I trust that God was able to work powerfully and effectively through a weak and broken vessel? Or was I too fixated on the issues and various leadership choices at hand to see that God himself had positioned Jay for this time? As Romans 14:4 teaches, *"Who are you to judge the servant of another? To his own master he stands or falls; and he will stand, for the Lord is able to make him stand."*

I threw my support behind Jay and served in any way he asked me to during this outreach. It paid off. Slowly, the other team members and even some of the local church leaders changed their attitudes and chose to unify around Jay's leadership. In the end, the project was an incredible success!

Not a smooth success, perhaps, but the purposes of God were accomplished and the team held together. We saw hundreds of young Russians transformed by the love of God, and due to the tremendous change in their young people, many of the churches repented of their infighting and came into solid unity. It was a huge win for the Kingdom of God in that area of the world. I have since learned that it is possible to trust Jesus in someone even when that individual may seem untrustworthy at a given time.

Your test may come in the form of having to support and serve under a leader who is less than ideal, or you may find that your *Right to be Right* rears its head like a dragon even in the midst of the small things in life. In my experience, this "Last Christian Right" has done more to damage teams and the overall efforts of the Kingdom than almost anything. Cherishing and asserting this "Last Christian Right" is nothing more than walking in pride. According to the word of God, *"Pride goes before destruction, And a haughty spirit before stumbling."* (Prov 16:18) If you walk in pride and assert your *Right to be Right* you will have allowed the enemy an inroad by which to invade your team, family or community. The devil will happily drive his vehicles of destruction down this road, right through the door of your heart, and wreak havoc on your life; and through you, he will bring destruction into the lives of those in your sphere of influence.

You may feel *right* and you might actually be *right*, but if you assert this *Right to be Right* you are partnering with destruction and setting yourself up to stumble.

So what to do? You have to cut off the head of this dragon and give up the *Right to be Right*. Lay it down at the cross and choose to reject this subtly disguised form of pride. God doesn't need you to be right and he doesn't need your *rightness* to accomplish His purposes. He needs your humility and submission. Often the walk of humility is a walk in weakness, either our own, or the weakness of others.

> *"But he said to me, 'My grace is sufficient for you, for my power is made perfect in weakness. Therefore I will boast all the more gladly about my weaknesses, so that Christ's power may rest on me.'"* (2 Cor 12:9)

Do you want to be a highway that brings the life of God into your sphere of influence? Then do not allow your pride to become a roadblock for what God wants to do through you. Be aware of this "Last Christian Right."

Often we don't correctly diagnose this *right* as a problem. Once aware, we can actively oppose the destructive dragon of pride and learn to die to ourselves by choosing the path of humility. In dying to ourselves, we find that we not only *truly* live, but also bring life to others.

Chapter 4
The Twinkie Principle

WE WERE STARVING. NEVER BEFORE HAD I imagined how hungry and thirsty a person could become. We had been nearly four days without a proper meal and even our meager supplies of clean drinking water had been used up. Our team of 40 teenagers and adult volunteers had been reduced to scavenging our way through Romania, living on canned prune juice and goat cheese.

1990 was a rough time in Eastern Europe. Our team found itself right in the middle of one of the most volatile seasons in the history of Western civilization. Our group of teenagers and adult chaperones were on a seven-week trip that had originated in the USA. We traveled to Vienna, Austria then to the beautiful Black Sea town of Yalta, in the Crimean region of Southern Ukraine. No one imagined how difficult it would be to complete this assignment. Our plan was to drive from Vienna, through Hungary and Romania, then on through the newly free, former Soviet Republic of Moldova. Once through Moldova we planned to drive in our undersized and overloaded bus along the coast of Ukraine to eventually reach Yalta.

This region is beautiful, and the facility at Artek was formerly the crown jewel of Soviet youth camps. Our plan was to allow for about nine days of driving on either side of a four-week stay at Artek. This was going to be a long, long drive, but when we made it successfully to Artek, we anticipated living in the midst of, and ministering directly to more than 20,000 Soviet youth who had never heard of Jesus. Needless to say, our team was tremendously excited. This was the first time a venture like this had been launched since the fall of the Berlin Wall, and it was definitely the first time a group of our size had made the attempt.

The entire region was experiencing various levels of social upheaval. The Soviet Union was fractured. The original countries that had formed this once-massive superpower were once again appearing. We first realized the challenges we were to face at the border between Austria and Hungary.

When our bus took our place in line and queued up for the border crossing, we found ourselves more than ten miles away from the actual checkpoint. We were stuck in a line of carbon-copy Soviet cars known as the "Lada." This line of cars was not moving. People had left their cars and had set up roadside camps as they waited, sometimes weeks, to be processed back into Hungary.

With the collapse of the Soviet Union, satellite countries, such as Hungary, were cut off from basic supplies of food and fuel. All of the people in our line had departed from Hungary to venture into Austria in order to purchase food and fuel. The idea was to return again to Hungary, bringing supplies to desperate family and friends back home.

However, once they were out of the country they found the understaffed border station assigned to manage the influx back into Hungary was overwhelmed by the returning exodus. Some of these lines had literally been parked and waiting weeks to cross. When we realized what was happening we thought our trip was going to be over before it had even begun. It seemed hopeless.

It was at this point that these pressures really began to take a toll on our team. As we sat trapped in our bus, looking at the miles of vehicles lined up before us, we decided the only option was to pray. This we did in earnest. In what become the first of many miracles on this outreach we saw a police vehicle pull up next to us and speak with our driver. Within minutes our bus was extracted from the traffic jam of the century and quickly brought to the very front of the line. Needless to say the stranded drivers of the other vehicles were understandably furious and began throwing things at our bus and yelling not so affirming exclamations in our direction. But the Lord was proving that He was with us and we were quickly moved through the border process and continued on into Romania. Sometimes you will find that our loving Father God will provide strong affirmations and confirmations before you enter into a time trials and testing.

Our circumstances worsened as we crossed the border into Romania. Six months earlier, the Romanian people had overthrown their communist dictator, Nicolae Ceaușescu. He had dominated Romania with an iron fist for decades and the country was falling apart. Food, clean water and basic supplies were nearly impossible to find and the Civil Government was almost non-existent at the time. Once you were in the country you were truly on your own, unless you were sheltered and guided by the Creator of the universe.

There was almost no food left in the country. As soon as our team leaders discovered this, they knew they had a problem on their hands. The problem was in the form of 35 hungry teenagers. Our team leaders began to alter our navigational plan. The new plan would take us through larger Romanian towns that might have enough food available to feed all of us. The leaders instructed our bus driver to call ahead to any known restaurants to inquire about the availability of food, and then to make our traveling plans accordingly.

Sadly, through the first two days there was no food or clean water available in any of the towns through which we passed. Our team members became grumpier as their bellies became emptier, and the daily temperatures soared above 90 degrees Fahrenheit. We began to make random stops at farms to buy homemade goat cheese to eat. The only form of liquid we could find to drink was in the form of gallon-sized cans of prune juice. So, not only were we incredibly hungry, but now we were also dealing with the effects of drinking straight prune juice all day!

On the third day, finally, we found a restaurant in a dusty little Romanian town and parked our bus in front. This establishment had promised us that they had meat to serve us, as well as hot tea. We were very excited and incredibly hungry. As soon as the plates of breaded, fried meat came out, all of us began to eat ravenously. But just as soon afterward, literal tears and weeping began among us as we realized the meat was actually undercooked slabs of cow liver. It was nearly inedible.

Following this traumatic dining experience, we headed back to our bus as the adults lingered in the restaurant to pay for the fried liver. As we approached the bus we noticed that a crowd of local Romanians had gathered around it. The large crowd, possibly 500 people, was armed with pitch forks, sticks, and other homemade weapons. They were not happy. The town was starving and this local restaurant had refused to sell them what little food they had because they hoped to sell it to us for an exorbitant price. The restaurant had claimed to have no food to sell to their townspeople, but now it was clear to the mob that they had been lied to and they decided to take their anger out on us.

We hurried through this agitated crowd and quickly loaded as many team members as possible onto the bus. But we didn't quite make it. Suddenly, the crowd exploded into a riot and the townspeople began bashing our bus with bottles and rocks. They violently tilted the bus from side to side as if to overturn it. One of the girls from our team was slow in getting through the bus door to safety. While she was still halfway in and halfway out, two strong Romanian men grabbed one of her arms and a frantic tug-of-war began, with this poor girl being used as the rope!

So much dust was flung into the air by the mob that we could hardly see what was happening. People were screaming as bottles and rocks were flying through the open windows of the bus. As we struggled to pull our team member fully through the door, I looked up to see one of our adult leaders running through the crowd at full speed like a powerful footballer. He too was a strong man and from the restaurant had seen that our teammate was in danger. With a right-hook to the jaw, thrown at a dead run, he hit the Romanian man who pulled on our girl. The man went down, knocked out cold. For a moment, the mob backed away from the bus door. We quickly boarded the rest of our team and our driver took the bus out of the parking area at full speed.

Amazingly, no one was seriously hurt and we had escaped the food riot. We didn't wait around to see what happened to the restaurant. This was a tough trip in a part of the world that was suffering tremendously. Needless to say, we were being squeezed by the vise of God. The content of our character was laid bare for all to see. Sadly, much that showed bore no resemblance to the character of Christ. Bitterness, anger, complaining, murmuring, divisive attitudes and open rebellion began to flow from people's hearts.

Following our escape from the angry mob we were still intensely hungry and thirsty. Sadly our prune juice had begun to ferment and we couldn't drink it. Having exited the city, we stopped the bus high up on a beautiful mountainside. We searched a promising area for running water, but found none. As I was rummaging through my duffel bag, one of the younger team members approached me. I had just found a small bottle of drinking water in my bag that I had forgotten about. He began to beg me desperately to sell him my bottle of water. He offered me twenty dollars, all of his spending money. I gave it to him without accepting his money. He was much more desperate than I was and I felt compelled by the Lord to just give him the water.

In the midst of adversity is where you have the chance to see miracles! Our bus had stopped at a scenic overlook located on top of a tall cliff. The view was spectacular. I could look for miles and miles at the beautiful country of Romania and onward into Moldova. Sadly, most of my teammates couldn't see past their immediate suffering and were unable to appreciate the view.

By this time we had passed six days with almost no food and most of the team had moved past the anger and complaining phase and were now simply wandering aimlessly, depressed and withdrawn. However, standing at the top of the cliff overlook I felt that it was time to celebrate. I had saved a small zip-lock bag of trail mix as my ultimate reserve of food. Now was the time to eat it; I was so hungry. I remember thinking that I might be mobbed by my team once they had seen this meager portion of food come out of my bag so I might as well share it right up front. I quietly prayed over it as I opened the bag. Mostly my prayer was that I would actually get to eat at least a few bites of my own food before it was devoured by dozens of famished teens.

I pulled out the trail mix and began quietly walking up to each of my teammates to offer them a portion. Most people took their handful greedily, without regard for sharing. Still, I felt God was in the moment and that I was being tested. As I continued to pass out the trail mix, I suddenly realized that I was in the middle of a quiet miracle. I was not running out of trail mix. The bag was not becoming empty. I almost tried to pretend that it wasn't happening. After I had given handfuls of trail mix to every person on my team I looked in my little bag and the level of the trail mix had only dropped by about one inch! I was so tired and hungry I could hardly think of what to do or how to praise God for this incredible miracle. I had just had my own *loaves and fishes* miracle and there was still a full bag of trail mix left for me to eat. I ate every last piece and the miracle ended. Most people had received enough trail mix to fill up their shrunken stomachs and stop their hunger pains.

"*I have told you these things, so that in me you may have peace. In this world you will have trouble. But take heart! I have overcome the world.*" (John 16:33)

Even when we have trouble in this life, we can still have peace because Jesus has overcome the world. Adversity can be used either for growth and refinement, or, if we respond negatively, it will serve as a mirror to reflect the condition of our souls. Either way, it is not without benefit to the servant of God.

The apostle Peter explains it this way. *"In this you greatly rejoice, even though now for a little while, if necessary, you have been distressed by various trials, so that the proof of your faith, being more precious than gold which is perishable, even though tested by fire,* **may be found to result** *in praise and glory and honor at the revelation of Jesus Christ . . . "*(1 Peter 1:6-7)

It is often said that character is created in adversity. In general, I agree with this statement. However, one phenomenon I have also found to be true is that adversity often serves to reveal what a person's character honestly is. Consider my analogy of squeezing a "Twinkie" brand snack cake: on the outside, in a nice little package, a Twinkie looks like a delicious little piece of cake. But if you take that Twinkie and give it a good squeeze you will quickly discover that there is something entirely different on the inside. A flattened Twinkie will produce white frosting all over your hands.

You are something like a Twinkie. On the undisturbed outside you may have one appearance, but if someone or something applies pressure to your life, another aspect of who you are may be revealed. While there may be some debate about the health benefits of the innards of a Twinkie, when *you* get squeezed, the "Character" that emerges will crystal clear. Whatever is already inside of you, the quality of your character, will be revealed for all to see. What will the result of your testing by fire be? Will it be, *"praise and glory and honor at the revelation of Jesus Christ?"*

Often we have no real idea what is inside of us. The truth about one's character, values and motives is rarely pressed to the point of exposure during the normal course of a comfortable existence. Adversity is God's primary tool used to expose the inner workings of a person's heart. It is possible to spend a whole lifetime building up walls of comfort and security behind which to hide ones true self. Each brick that is placed into that personal wall is an action calculated to prevent exposure. In the adversity we experience, God breaks the brick wall so that portions of one's life, where necessary, may be tested by fire. This is part of the sanctification process in our lives. The challenge for every believer is to embrace the scorching and to honestly assess the aftermath. If parts of your character don't survive the scorching wind of adversity then these areas needed to be focused on. The Bible says that we are being transformed, and transformation comes from a lot of 'squishing.'

"And do not be conformed to this world, but be transformed by the renewing of your mind, so that you may prove what the will of God is, that which is good and acceptable and perfect."(Romans 12:2)

"Consider it all joy, my brethren, when you encounter various trials, knowing that the testing of your faith produces endurance. And let endurance have its perfect result, so that you may be perfect and complete, lacking in nothing."(James 1:2-4)

The *various trials* mentioned by James refer to the scorching that comes into our lives. This testing of our faith is the only way we discover what really is inside of us. The goal of all adversity, trial, or character testing is transformation. God wants us to be transformed by the renewing of our minds. There can be no transformation unless first we recognize that things already formed need to be reformed. Our character is not already *conformed* to the likeness of Christ. However, through our trials that Christ-likeness is coming to be.

According to James the key to this process is to "consider it all joy," when we have to endure trials and testing. Joy gives us the ability to embrace the adversity that comes to us in life. Endurance is really the act of embracing adversity. If we chose joy we will not only see ourselves transformed, but at the end we will find ourselves complete and lacking nothing. Each of us wants to be made perfect and complete. Each of us desires a life where we lack nothing. James promises us that if we let endurance have its perfect work we will gain these things.

Adversity is one factor that acts on the 'ship of your life' much like a strong wind effects a sailing ship. Trials and adversity are like a wind that hits the sails of your life. Your life, like a ship, is driven by many factors. Forces that we encounter such as adversity can be helpful in exposing your heading. The direction your life is already aiming toward. Just as with a sailing ship, the wind that you encounter will begin to push you in a direction. The question is what direction is your ship going to move in once it is given a good push?

Now, how do you harness the power of adversity and let it aim the 'Ship of Life' toward spiritual perfection and completion? Your ship has to have a strong rudder and in our metaphor, a strong rudder is a way of depicting strong personal character. Your character is what enables you to harness the driving winds of adversity. Your character is not neutral, but has been slowly shaped over time and aimed in a particular direction due to the compounding of choices throughout your life. So when the wind of adversity forces your ship to move, your rudder (your character) automatically determines the direction that this force will drive your ship (the direction of your life).

God cares deeply about your ships destination. The direction your ship begins to move once the pressure of adversity has been applied allows you to see with greater clarity the direction you were already headed. The only way to correct the course of your ship is to first allow God to show you where it is already heading, and then to alter your course as may be required. Therefore, adversity can become a useful ally when you allow it to be God's tool of course-correction *before* you crash your life on a reef.

Chapter 5
Making the Most of it

"Be wise in the way you act toward outsiders; make the most of every opportunity." (Colossians 4:5)

I HAVE HIKED ON MANY MOUNTAIN PATHS. The Rocky Mountains of North America and the Himalayas are my two favorite areas. One thing a successful hiker learns is to never give up altitude. Once you have worked hard and trekked hard to obtain a certain elevation on the mountain, you are very careful to keep it, and to keep moving upward. Hikers do not carelessly work their way back down hill; they only do so when there is a very real need.

The enemy of your soul also plays by this rule. He will not willingly give up any high ground or advantage he has attained in any given cultural location. He does not easily yield to the Kingdom of God. In an effort to hold his ground, one of the many weapons he will hurl at an outreach team is disillusionment.

I have observed and been part of many outreach efforts over the years in which the team members began to suffer from disillusionment. Sometimes there are feelings of "let down" soon after arriving at the outreach location; there is often such a build-up of spiritual and emotional energy leading up to a Kingdom assignment that when finally on-site, the realities of facing the new environment can be overwhelming. Additionally, ministry teams may run full-force into any of the following realities:

1. The people the team is trying to reach love their sin, or are not interested in the Gospel.
2. No well-organized ministry activities have been arranged.
3. Strategy and outreach methods don't seem to be effective or relevant to the population at hand.
4. The front-line people the team has come to support seem disorga-

nized or uninterested.
5. Living conditions are extremely difficult and basic survival consumes all of the team's time.
6. The team can find no point of interpersonal or intercultural connection with the people they are attempting to engage.
7. The language barrier is insurmountable.

All of the above can be summed up in this over-arching theme: I spent all this money and gave up so much time to be here but there are no opportunities to advance the Kingdom.

As real as these and other oppositional factors may seem to be, it is important to remember that God has brought you to this location, to this project, and into this season in spiritual history for, "such a time as this." (Esther 4:14) He did not make a mistake by involving you in His Kingdom work, so be prepared to hold your ground against the, "fiery darts," of disillusionment. (Eph 6:16)

In years of Kingdom work, I have learned that there is always opportunity. God has something amazing in mind and it is the joy of His royal children to figure it out by connecting with the heart of their father.

Often the events we perceive as challenges and difficulties are just part of the way our heavenly father, the King of the Universe, invites his children into his work. He wants to treat you as a co-heir with Christ. You are royalty. You are princes and princesses in the Kingdom of God. When your heavenly father sends you into a difficult assignment you can rejoice because he is trusting you with part of your inheritance in advance! God wants to raise you up to be like Jesus. You are to be conformed to the image of Christ. One of the ways you become like Christ is to manage the father's property just as the father would.

Jesus said, *"Truly, truly, I say to you, the Son can do nothing of Himself, unless it is something He sees the Father doing; for whatever the Father does, these things the Son also does in like manner."* (John 5:19)

Why does it often seem that God *conceals a matter* from us when we are in the midst of truly difficult circumstances? After all, He sent us into these assignments, it was His idea, so why is the best path often so unclear? I believe he conceals things *not* so that we will be harmed or disillusioned, but instead, that we will be passionately motivated to seek out what is on his heart. What things has God concealed from you?

The Lord conceals matters from you so that you will find them. You find *them* by finding *Him*. God wants to find out if you value what he values. What better way for God to test the heart of a man but to see what you desire to discover in life? Do you seek out his hidden treasures or do you spend your time, treasure, and talent seeking out the things of this world?

Looking at what Jesus said in John 5:19, it is clear that we, like Jesus, can do no Kingdom work that is simply originates as your own idea. However, when we seek out what seems to be concealed we then find what the father is doing.

What did we see Jesus do in His life and ministry? We find Him often at the center of the "scene." Even when there wasn't a scene, Jesus was not afraid to make a scene. He was not timid, he was not fearful; he was definitely not intimidated by cultural considerations. He had seen what the Father was doing and He was going to do that, *in like manner*. If there isn't a scene, then you need to find out what God is doing and partner with the Holy Spirit to make a scene!

You cannot expect the devil to easily give up any of the high ground that he has taken in a culture or a people group, but God wants you to take back that territory from the enemy and force him to lose altitude and influence in your outreach location. Your assignment is to seek out what is in God's heart for that people, that time and that place, and to do that, "in like manner." There is no excuse for boredom in the Kingdom of God! There is too much to be done, and there is too much power available to us as co-heirs with Christ Jesus to ever justify a mundane Christian life.

Sometimes your initial strategy won't work out and you'll need to adjust your plan.

Our team was sitting around the small living room space in our 1940's, refugee housing in central Ukraine. We were a team of 18 people from all over the world. Shortly after the collapse of the Soviet Union we had come to bring healing and the gospel message to the Ukrainian people.

We had been conducting open air, evangelistic events on streets and plazas for nearly six weeks. Often we conducted three events per day, walking more than four miles in between event locations. The Lord was moving so profoundly among the people in that season that we thought it was a slow day if fewer than 1000 people came to the Lord in repentance.

Now, however, things were really slow. Our local facilitators and partners had run out of ideas and we were struggling to figure out what was next. We did not want to waste even a day of this incredible opportunity in spiritual history. God had entrusted these events to us. As we sought the Lord for what was next, we were thinking only of traditional evangelistic approaches. As we prayed about what to do, someone on the team remembered hearing about the dire conditions facing Ukrainians who required mental health care.

The next scene we were going to make struck at the heart of darkness in this community. We approached the rusty iron gate at the front of a mental hospital as a large group.

During the Soviet phase of control over Ukraine many people were committed to mental hospitals or "asylums" whenever they exhibited issues that traditional medical hospitals could not understand or manage. Often, these issues were spiritual in nature, but the atheistic worldview of the medical community did not have a means for dealing with the violent and tormented condition that afflicted many citizens. Therefore, the only recourse conceivable to them was to commit these afflicted members of society to an asylum, thereby keeping them away from the rest of the community.

A local pastor explained this dynamic to us in detail, and mentioned that he wished he could do something to help these people, particularly at one local asylum. His prayers for a way to respond were answered through our team. After praying and seeking the Lord for direction about what to do next, we felt strongly that we should invite ourselves to this local asylum to share the Gospel and minister in the area of healing. It was time to make a scene. Obviously the devil was not going to hand over any of his captives willingly, so it was time to take back some high ground.

It was time for us to deal violently with the powers of darkness and take ground for the Kingdom by spiritual force.

When we approached the gate our group was dressed in performance clothing and costumes; some of us had white face makeup on... we were a disconcerting sight for the average, sheltered Ukrainian. When we arrived at the gate and asked to be let in it probably appeared to the guards that we were there to check ourselves in as patients! They had never seen anything like this before. I think they opened the gates out of a sense of humorous disbelief, but to us it was like the Red Sea parting and we went into the complex.

As our leaders negotiated with the administration of the asylum, we stood around observing this bleak and hopeless facility. The entrance was a dark grey concrete with steel bars covering the few visible windows. It looked more like the entrance to a nuclear bunker than a hospital. Negotiations were over in a few minutes and the amazed administration agreed to gather all the patients into an indoor, central amphitheater so we could perform and share. This was probably the first entertainment that had ever made its way into a Soviet asylum!

As we made our way into the amphitheater I realized we were in for a wild time. More than 500 patients were herded into the bleacher-style seats and the administrators were quickly organizing them into sections and rows. It was tumultuous and out of the control of the facility staff. People were screaming, fighting and wandering around in a way that you might think could only be portrayed in a movie.

As soon as the administration had organized and seated the crowd, the administrators disappeared. Every administrator made a fast exit from the auditorium before we had even established ourselves on the large stage at the front of the auditorium. It was obvious that they were not confident that this gathering was going to go well. Then I felt something hit me in the back and turned around to see a syringe with an exposed needle laying on the ground. Quickly, I felt all around my back where I'd felt the impact and had one of my team members check for any puncture wound. By God's grace the plunger end of the syringe had hit me instead of the needle! Who knows what diseases could have been carried by that syringe.

As syringes and other random objects continued to fly in all directions, it was clear to me why the administration had wanted to be out of that room. We were beginning to question whether we had heard the Lord clearly on this idea. As quickly as we could, we began our performance and intermittently shared testimonies from our own lives about the work that God had done in each of our lives. No one was listening. It was chaos in the seats and a number of people in the crowd were beginning to manifest demons, as well. This frightened their fellow patients and increased the disorder.

Finally, our team leader said, "this isn't working." For what comes next, I should explain in advance that we had one translator with our team at this event: our team leader's wife was from a Ukrainian family in the USA and spoke both the English and Ukrainian. Our team leader continued, by saying, "Ok, let's just pray for them to be healed." He had us all stand at the front of the stage, lined up with the descending stairways that led down from the bleachers. He said, "I'm going to call them to come forward if they want to be healed and you guys are going to pray for them!"

Not only was this incredibly intimidating, but none of us spoke Ukrainian. I mentioned this detail to him as we got ourselves positioned for what was gearing up to be one of the wildest prayer events I had ever seen. Our team leader said, "Don't worry about it, God will tell you what to pray for and they will be healed." So it began. The announcement went out to come down if you wanted to be healed. They came in a rush. Long lines formed down the stairways and hundreds of the patients waited for prayer.

The first person I encountered was a young man who seemed to be fairly normal in appearance but had a very sad countenance. I found out later that his own family had him locked up in this asylum when he began to suffer from demonic oppression at night. It prevented him from sleeping. As he stood before me I laid a hand on his shoulder and just prayed out, "Lord, I don't know what is wrong with this guy, but whatever it is, I ask that you would heal him in Jesus' name." That was all I had. Suddenly, the guy began to shrug his shoulders and shake out his limbs like someone warming for a boxing match.

Through his excited charades we figured out that he had suffered from pain or arthritis in all of his joints, but after we prayed, the pain was gone! He quickly ran up the stairs to where one of his friends was sitting and proceeded to bodily drag the unwilling man down to us to have him prayed for as well. The man did not initially cooperate, but after a quick prayer over him he was healed as well! We had no idea what he was healed from, but the two of them immediately ran from the auditorium! We learned later that they had checked themselves out of the hospital and their families had come to take them home.

All over the front of the auditorium similar scenes were being repeated with our other team members laying hands on people and seeing them healed. Our one translator was running from healing to healing, confirming what had happened and asking if those that were healed wanted to receive Christ. It was an amazing situation. I lost my voice from praying for so many people. Hundreds were healed and many received Christ. Sometime after midnight we finally finished praying for the last person. My head was spinning, and I was completely voiceless and exhausted. Our team was flying high on this incredible experience with Jesus.

We found out later that a large percentage of the patients at the asylum were delivered and healed. Many of them had then gone on to check themselves out of the hospital and return home to their families. This is God's desire and compassion for humanity: That we be healed, delivered, and made whole. As a prince or princess in the Kingdom of God, there is never a reason to be bored. If there isn't an obvious set of opportunities to advance the Kingdom, then lay hold of it forcefully and make a scene.

Chapter 6
You Get Out What You Put In

"Remember this: Whoever sows sparingly will also reap sparingly, and whoever sows generously will also reap generously." (2 Cor 9:6)

I HAVE LISTENED TO MANY POST-OUTREACH DEBRIEFINGS. I have listened to many teams in the midst of outreach and received their reports. Over the years I began to see a noticeable difference in their reports. Individuals told their own stories about one of their shared team experiences but the accounts were as different from each other as night and day. While one person shared of the miraculous, another shared of the mundane. One person shared of the power of God delivering someone from bondage to sin while the other person recounted the problems with food and air-conditioning. Another person would share of seeing angels but his teammate shared of seeing dysfunction in the team.

It is amazing that so frequently people in the midst of the same experiences can have such differing perspectives. There is a timeless principle that God has built into the very fabric of the universe. This is the principle of Sowing and Reaping (Gal 6:7). Like the other laws of the universe that God has established, it was designed for your blessing. You sow a seed, you reap a plant for food; when you sow love, you can reap a loving response; when you sow to righteousness, you reap a blessing. For this principle to legitimately work there has to be the possibility of a negative outcome. A truth is not true unless the opposite is false.

"Whoever sows to please their flesh, from the flesh will reap destruction; whoever sows to please the Spirit, from the Spirit will reap eternal life." (Gal 6:8)

This principle of sowing and reaping is very real and is intended to benefit you and the people you influence. The ultimate goal of God's design is the "reaping of eternal life." When you are serving in a Kingdom assignment you are being entrusted with the opportunity to sow seeds that will produce a harvest, a harvest of "eternal life." You can look at your sowing and reaping in another way as well. It can be viewed as an investment.

As a young believer I discovered the truth of the principle of sowing and reaping in the context of Kingdom fieldwork. Not everyone will personally invest at the same level nor will all see the same return on their investment. I'm not talking about finances. I am referring to eternal investment, the investment of your time, treasure, and talent as led by the Holy Spirit. I learned of this truth on my first field assignment overseas. In 1988 when I was 14 years old, my parents arranged for me to join a group of 50 other teenagers on an outreach to the Philippines and China. We had many amazing experiences during this summer-long trip.

The government of China hosted our team and allowed us to conduct daily musical performances of worship songs. We performed in schools all around the Beijing area. Even at 14 years old I was able to grasp the magnitude of this opportunity. However, as is often the case among groups of young believers, insecurity and inexperience governed most of our decisions. The one thing I had going for me was that I knew my God and I also knew that all people need to know there is freedom from sin through the gift of Jesus Christ.

Our first large event took place in a high school auditorium. The school officials had brought together thousands of students to hear our presentation and enjoy our musical performance. In these days in China there was almost no opportunity for their citizens to see a spectacle like us. Foreigners were extremely rare then, so seeing more than 50 of us at once, on stage, was quite an experience for these young Chinese.

At the beginning of this first large-scale event, our team leaders had asked for several of us to share our testimonies and greet the students at the end of the event. At this request, most of us looked like deer in the headlights of a car: *scared stiff*. Slowly and carefully five of us raised our hands. I had just volunteered to remain on stage after the rest of the team moved off at the end of the performance. When the performance was complete, this small group stood before a crowd of thousands of cheering and clapping Chinese students.

Although I had never done anything like this before, I was gripped by the eternal magnitude of the opportunity. Someone handed me a microphone and as I looked around, side to side, to see what my teammates were doing,

I saw ... no one. Every one of them had scampered off the stage and left me standing there alone. All eyes were on me and I was overwhelmed. This is not exactly how you want to start your first public speaking experience! However, God's grace was there for me. Honestly, the thought of just bowing to the audience and then sprinting offstage like everyone else, did cross my mind, but I decided to stay and share.

For five minutes I stood on a stage before thousands of students, in a land where Christianity was outlawed, and shared about God's love and His work in my life. It was likely these precious eternal souls had never heard such a message before. Then I walked off the stage. By God's grace, not only had I survived being, "thrown to the lions," in this opportunity, but also I had learned an early lesson about taking risks. An investment is always a risk but you must invest if you want to see a return. Sharing my testimony was an investment into the spiritual future of these students but I was facing a real possibility that they would not receive what I had to say or that I could even be laughed at by the crowd.

Like me, you may feel that you've only been given limited ability or a small amount of resources, and that you don't have anything to contribute. Perhaps you are like the person who received only one "talent" in the famous parable that Jesus shared in Matthew 25:14-29. In this parable, one servant received five talents, or measures, of money from his master; another received two, and the last servant of the master received one talent. The master then went away to a far country for a while.

When he returned, he met with the three servants to find out what they did with the money he gave them. The first two servants invested the money they received, and so were able to give back to their master not only the original investment, but more also. They were quickly found faithful and responsible, so the master put them in charge of cities in accordance with the measure of their faithfulness and ability. However, the last servant, who had only received the one talent from the master, was afraid. He took the one talent and hid it in the ground, and then gave it back to the master when he returned.

The master was greatly displeased: not that the servant with one talent had not produced five talents with it, but that the servant had not at least invested it in the bank so that it would have produced a small amount of interest. All our master is looking for is a faithful use of whatever resource he has given us. We all have some measure of Time, Treasure and Talent that we can invest in Kingdom purposes. What we do with the little we have has eternal implications. Not only for the people we are to reach, but also for our future reward in the eternal Kingdom of God.

When you become involved in Kingdom endeavors, such as a short-term missions outreach, you will find yourself right in the middle of a golden opportunity to invest what you have been given. You will be able to give back to your Master, Jesus, whatever He has entrusted to you, along with the increase of His eternal reward (Hebrews 12:2), the salvation of the lost and hurting ones He died to rescue. Proper stewardship of the abundant life God has given us is the one of the most practical and daily expressions of worship that one can offer to the Lord.

Here are a few key ideas that will help give depth and perspective to any Kingdom endeavor that you set your hand to:

1. Outreach, or any other God-given opportunity, is what you and God together make of it.
2. You get out what you put in and sometimes a lot more.
3. If you love, your heart will break as does God's heart.
4. If you immerse yourself in the season and circumstances God has called you into you will engage.
5. If you dive into the context and challenges presented you will be changed.
6. If you invest you will reap a reward for the Kingdom.

However, conversely, if you risk nothing you will reap nothing and you will find that a conduit for God's love and mercy has been closed off to the needy world that surrounds you.

Later on in my ministry life, when I was 19 years old and on my first major overseas field assignment and I was not what you would call an accomplished public speaker. Nor was I overly confident in my ability to share a cohesive or comprehensive overview of the Gospel. But I knew the Lord and I was confident in Him and his ability to work through any willing servant. I felt like I had only "one small talent," to invest yet I resolved that God would receive a return on His investment in me.

During this 1993 field assignment, our team was deep in the heart of Ukraine. This newly liberated country was in a state of upheaval as it attempted to reassert its identity apart from the recently collapsed Soviet Union. In the midst of this time of great suffering and lack there was also a great spiritual awakening happening. Our three-month field assignment was during one of the greatest moments of harvest that has ever happened in the Kingdom of God. Our daily schedule of activities featured a series of two or three evangelism and healing events.

On the flip-side of God's amazing work on the one hand, was our daily need to eat, and that meant a kind of daily scavenging. Food was so scarce that I had the dubious honor of regularly standing in Soviet-era breadlines in the Ukraine, hoping to be given a ration of freshly baked bread. Sometimes these lines were six hours long! All of this effort usually produced only one loaf of dense, brown bread: it was wonderful bread, though! Sometimes, after finally reaching the distribution window, the Ukrainian women who distributed the bread realized that we were young Americans. Probably a mixture of shame for their country's condition, and pity for us, led more than one of them to slip an extra loaf of bread into our ration bags and to insist that we take it.

During this adventure, I discovered that many of my teammates were extremely reluctant to risk investing the talents that God had entrusted to them. Whether from fear or insecurity or lack of commitment, they unanimously resisted either sharing their testimonies or sharing the Gospel when asked to do so. We had three outreach events happening on most days. By the end of the first week of observing my team leader's struggle to motivate us to share, I finally volunteered. I couldn't bear to see these historic opportunities not maximized for the Kingdom! So I finally told my team leader, "If no one else wants to share, then I will share at every event." He happily agreed.

I quickly became the default preacher for the team, even though my "preaching" was generally limited to a basics of the Gospel message. Imagine my surprise when by his grace and empowerment it worked! Investing my one talent began to produce great increase. Soon, we were seeing thousands of people come to the Lord in deep repentance, and many of them were immediately healed and delivered.

As the outreach continued I knew that I had made the right decision. I would not bury my one talent, instead I would take a risk and invest it. By the end of this three-month field assignment we had lived miracles, and I had the privilege of sharing our risen, victorious Savior and the love of God with tens of thousands of these wonderful Ukrainian people. Of these, thousands had responded to the message and had entered into relationship with the Savior of their Souls.

Don't bury your one talent. Take a risk and invest it, looking forward to the time when you can offer it back to your Master along with its Kingdom increase. The Time, Treasure and Talent that God has given you is your modern day equivalent of the "talents of money" that are mentioned in the Parable of the Talents. Now is your opportunity to be found faithful — a good steward of the Master's resources.

Chapter 7
Success is to Serve

As I stood in the doorway of a partially destroyed crumbling resort complex in southern Albania, I was slowly coming to terms with what I had heard the Lord say to me. Our team had just arrived in this coastal community. Our mission was to conduct four weeks of discipleship youth camps. We anticipated that more than 300 Albanian students from churches all over Albania would be participating. It was perfect summer weather and we had a gathered a vibrant team of volunteers to serve and minister to these students.

The problems began immediately upon arrival. As soon as we and our Albanian hosts arrived at the complex, we discovered the facilities had been padlocked; closed due to an ongoing legal dispute between the land owners. The person in charge of the facility apologized and proceeded to show us another nearby facility that we could use. The second facility was an abandoned, run-down version of the original facility, and had not been used in at least a decade. However, we had no choice. 300 students were arriving in 12 hours, and there was no way to call off the program or change the location.

Cell phones were not an option in those days; neither was the internet. Communication was impossible and most of the students were already in buses on their way! The facility we were relegated to was in dismal condition. Windows were broken, doors didn't work, bathrooms were backed up and overflowing. The bunk rooms were filled with wet and rotting bedding. Worse yet there were no showers! The students would later dub the facility, "Camp POW," or camp, "Prisoner of War." In the end result, God moved powerfully during the course of these programs and through many miracles, we not only survived but we thrived. The conditions were extremely bad, and intensely challenged the character of each of us.

I was charged with scouting the facility to determine what we needed to do to make the place livable for our students and volunteers. The primary focus of my task was to locate anything that could be used as a shower facility. I finally found it, or what was left of it…

When living near your home in your home country it is easy to pray strong prayers of commitment and pledge to obey or do anything you imagine that God might ask of you. However, when you find yourself face-to-face with the dire physical conditions, you may quickly find your vows to the Lord challenged. I did. As I stood in what had once been a doorway to a shower room, I was overwhelmed with disgust at what I saw. The room was about 15 feet by 20 feet, with one window opening, and was literally buried under the rubble of the broken-down second floor of the building. The window and door had been blown off in an explosion during one of Albania's many violent conflicts. It was also apparent this room had been used as an open toilet for many years. The floor of the room was covered by inches deep human waste. The smell was horrific and my eyes watered from the fumes even as I stood in the doorway.

What is the secret to success in any Kingdom enterprise? It is to be among mankind as "one who serves."

> *"And He said to them, "The kings of the Gentiles lord it over them; and those who have authority over them are called 'Benefactors.' But it is not this way with you, but the one who is the greatest among you must become like the youngest, and the leader like the servant. For who is greater, the one who reclines at the table or the one who serves? Is it not the one who reclines at the table? But I am among you as the one who serves."(Luke 22: 25-27)*

My quest to find our shower facility was over, and this was all there was. I could see shower nozzles in the far wall and it appeared that water was dripping from them. There was no way to check other than to walk through the waste that covered the floor, but at the moment I was not willing to do that. Now we had only eight hours until the first group of students were scheduled to arrive, and we had no way to provide showers for more than 300 people who would be coming through our programs that summer.

As I stood staring into the nightmarish room, I began to realize that *someone* was going to have to restore this facility. That is when God clearly spoke to me and said, "You are going to clean it." It took a few minutes for that instruction to sink in and process inside my heart. I began to remember fateful prayers I had prayed back home such as, "God, I'll go anywhere and do anything you want me to do!" Well, here I was, facing one of the worst potential "anythings" that could be asked of me. At that moment I made a crucial life decision: I chose to serve.

Approaching the world around us as a servant is like deploying a virus into the computer code that the devil uses to operate his destructive system of governance on the planet. The Bible refers to this system as "the World." This is why Jesus clearly instructed his disciples (us) regarding how to live and operate in this fallen world system. Our goal is to completely undermine the devil's work on the planet

Jesus made it very clear that we are not to be like the Kings of the Gentiles who use their authority to lord it over other people. We are to live life and thrive in our identity as "one who serves." The under appreciated secret weapon of servant-hood can not only reorder and align the world around you to the ways of God, but it can also determine who finds great favor with God.

Some of my team members had been exploring with me, looking for shower facilities, and when we found them, they quickly concluded, "God must not want us to shower this summer." They walked away. Standing alone in the doorway to this hellish, revolting, reeking room, I had a sense that this moment would profoundly influence my future. Would I obey? Would I take on the role of a servant? Or was I too good for that?

Once I had resolved in my heart to serve and obey, I hunted around and found the only tools available. I tied a bandanna around my face and took up two badminton rackets and waded into the shower room. Words cannot express how bad the smell was. I was walking in the muck wearing only my sport sandals and shoveling load after load of waste out the door using only my two badminton racket shovels. I piled the waste onto cardboard sheets at the door and dragged it to the dump-site about 50 yards away. This became the lowest point of my short missions career, but as I began to joyfully clean and restore this facility it became the high point of my service in the Kingdom.

Often it is what takes you low that actually sets you on high. This is the way Jesus chose to approach our fallen world, and to this day I am glad that I chose the humble, lowly route of servant obedience at such a young age. As I worked for hours, shoveling, scrubbing and spraying out this facility, team members would often come by and observe. They wanted to see first-hand what they had heard through rumor. One friend even wanted to bring in a video camera to film this awful situation, but he only lasted 30 seconds. He was overwhelmed with nausea and had to run. I was on my own, but now, that was ok. I had an overwhelming sense that God was receiving great pleasure watching me serve in this way and I wouldn't trade that moment for the world.

An hour before the students arrived, the shower hall was reclaimed. I had even constructed partitions from carefully tacked-up bed sheets to provide a bit of privacy and dignity in an environment that generally robbed its occupants of both. That shower hall ended up being the most heavily used part of our crumbling facility. Not only were many people blessed through my act of serving and obedience, but I sensed a promotion in the spiritual realm. I felt as though God was saying, "now I know that you will do anything I ask you to do." I also felt that this awful task had become an opportunity for me to not just sing worship to God but to actually perform worship to Him through the work of my hands.

Writing to the first century Corinthian church the Apostle Paul said, *"Now we have received, not the spirit of the world, but the Spirit who is from God, so that we may know the things freely given to us by God."* (1 Cor 2:12)

We are allowed a choice about which spirit will be allowed to govern our lives: The spirit of the world or the Spirit, "who is from God". These two very different spirits can be compared to very different operating systems on a computer.

The particular world system you align yourself with, through your thoughts and actions, will work towards establishing one kingdom or the other in your sphere of influence. In day to day living, as well as in the midst of a special outreach assignment, the goal remains the same. As Jesus prayed, *"Thy Kingdom come, Thy will be done, on earth as it is in Heaven."* (Matt 6:10)

Ultimately the goals of both kingdoms are spiritual. The conflict between the work of Christ and the assertions of authority by the enemy all hinge on who will have the worship of men. Whoever has a man's worship has his soul.

What is the source code of Heaven?

God designed the universe and he knows best how to govern it. To continue the computer metaphor, God has created the hardware (the universe), and He has also designed the original values system and worldview that will best govern His creation. God's system is clearly articulated throughout the entire narrative of scripture. When Paul says in Romans 12:2 "*And do not be conformed to this world, but be transformed by the renewing of your mind, so that you may prove what the will of God is, that which is good and acceptable and perfect,*" he is urging us to align our thoughts and actions in the same way that software must be compatible and aligned with the intended hardware platform in order to function.

Paul gave us a clear list of many elements in the value system or 'source code' for the operating system of the Kingdom of Heaven. Carefully note his instruction, "*But the fruit of the Spirit is love, joy, peace, patience, kindness, goodness, faithfulness, gentleness, self-control . . .* "These indicators will be present in the life of the believer who is aligned with the operating system of Heaven. Having a servant heart is one of the secret pieces of heaven's source code that overcomes the operating system of this world and enables you to influence the natural and spiritual realms that are around you.

What is the source code of the World System?

The World System is dominated by the, "spirit that is now working in the sons of disobedience." Ephesians 2:1-2 says, "*And you were dead in your trespasses and sins, in which you formerly walked according to the course of this world, according to the prince of the power of the air, of the spirit that is now working in the sons of disobedience.*"The Apostle Paul makes it clear that we cannot, as Christians, walk in the course of this world. We can think of Paul's use of the term, "the course of this world," as a first-century equivalent to our concept of a computer operating system. In scripture, there are some clearly articulated warnings about what constitutes the source code of the 'course of this world' or world system. Paul says in Galatians that if you align with this source code you are ultimately incompatible with the source code of heaven.

"Now the deeds of the flesh are evident, which are: immorality, impurity, sensuality, idolatry, sorcery, enmities, strife, jealousy, outbursts of anger, disputes, dissensions, factions, envying, drunkenness, carousing, and things like these, of which I forewarn you, just as I have forewarned you, that those who practice such things will not inherit the kingdom of God." (Gal 5:19-21)

The worldly operating system is that which the devil created and uses to rule much of the world. The enemy is primarily able to achieve his goals due to the choices sinners make to align with the enemy of their souls by using that system.

However, when you install the Holy-Spirit-empowered "virus" of *serving others* the devil's operating system doesn't know how to handle that code! Serving others "locks up" the system that the enemy created to keep Jesus out of peoples lives. Servanthood is your secret weapon in any situation or assignment. If you are "one who serves," you will short-circuit the carefully crafted defenses that the enemy has put in place. You will find yourself in a place of favor and influence that may seem completely unlikely in the eyes of the outside observer.

In certain Christian circles, the traditional discussion of this concept is called, "Moving in the Opposite Spirit." Scripture illustrates this principle simply and clearly. *"Bless those who persecute you; bless and do not curse.'"* (Rom 12:14) This is a foundational principle of spiritual victory!

Through intentionally choosing to live in opposition to the ideas, or the spiritual strongholds the enemy has created, we undermined the very foundation of darkness and align our God given strength with the Kingdom of Heaven. We undermine the claims and lies of the, "prince of the power of the air," (Eph 2:2) by consciously choosing to move in the opposite spirit. Moving in the opposite spirit will lead the believer in spiritual victory over the system of this world, and will keep them free from oppression.

Each day, you have a fresh chance to align with the operating system of heaven and to functionally negate and undermine the claims of the enemy in a given region or area of society. If you find that a society or a region of the world is steeped in control, dictatorship, or "lording it over others," then move in the opposite spirit. Align yourself with Jesus, the author of the source code of heaven, and serve! You will short-circuit the world's system and inject the fruit of the Spirit into a desperately needy and hurting world.

Which operating system will you choose?

Will you choose the system created by the enemy that is designed on the foundation of pride and selfishness? Or choose the original operating system designed by God for all of His creation that which, "is good and acceptable and perfect?" (Rom 12:2) Each system directly reflects the character and nature of its author. We are commanded to be transformed by the renewing of our minds so that we begin to reflect the character and nature of God. Scripture indicates that being transformed by the renewing of our mind will prove what the will of God is for all of creation.

A transformed follower of Jesus who has renewed his or her mind will take on the characteristics of Jesus. A true follower will think like Jesus and act like Jesus. In the context of this discussion we are considering Jesus' exhortation to become servants to all. Just as he served us, even to the point of his own, excruciating death. Everything about Jesus life, death and resurrection was about serving the undeserving. When we take on his Spirit we are able to short-circuit the world's system, just as Jesus did.

At times you may find yourself in a location or Kingdom assignment in which you are surrounded by nothing but suffering, difficulty and confusion. You may feel overwhelmed, and this can lead to feeling inadequate in the face of the challenges around you. The secret is to serve. If you can apply this one piece of source code, this one part of God's operating system, you will be a pleasing reminder to God of the lifestyle of Jesus and you will find unmerited favor with the people around you.

One of the main reasons serving is so powerful is that you have the choice to do otherwise. Jesus had the choice to do otherwise as well. He said, *"For who is greater, the one who reclines at the table or the one who serves? Is it not the one who reclines at the table? But I am among you as the one who serves."* (Luke 22:27)

Although He is greater, and is the one who one could expect to recline at the table being served, instead He chose otherwise. He chose to come humbly as a servant. *"The son of Man did not come to be served but to serve, and to give his life as a ransom for many."* (Matt 20:28)

The power of having options, the gift of choice, or free will, is by God's design. It might seem easy to obey or make a certain choice if there is no other option or alternative. However, it is the option to choose that defines your destiny. God wants you to have these options so that you have a legitimate choice. When you have a legitimate choice and you still choose Him, that is how you gain the favor of God.

You are adopted as sons and daughters by the King of Kings therefore you are brothers and sisters of Christ Himself. You may be entitled the option to recline at the table and not to serve... but if you intend to follow the example of Christ and want to see the world changed, you must choose to serve.

Chapter 8
Stay Usable

SUCCESSFUL OUTREACHES LARGELY DEPEND UPON THE SUCCESS of each individual member of the team. A team, much like a chain, is only as strong as its weakest link. One danger a team may face in any Kingdom enterprise is to ignore or marginalize the struggling members of the group. Unlike the self-centered and self-promoting teams one finds in the world's system, you are called to be concerned for the weak and vulnerable in your midst. Jesus is our model for doing life well, and Jesus never gave up on people or left them to the mess of their own making.

As a member of a godly team of Christians who are seeking to advance the Kingdom, you are called to do everything possible to take responsibility for each other, and to make sure there are no broken links in the chain of your team structure so that you all cross the finish line together. On the other hand, if, when you cross the finish line, you see behind you a trail of broken people, broken links in the chain, then you have not finished well. Your fellow team members are people that God has entrusted to you and you are responsible for their success just as much as you are responsible for whatever task God has given to your team. If you fail with the people that God has entrusted to you, then where is the reward in simply accomplishing a task?

> "Make my joy complete by being of the same mind, maintaining the same love, united in spirit, intent on one purpose. Do nothing from selfishness or empty conceit, but with humility of mind regard one another as more important than yourselves; do not merely look out for your own personal interests, but also for the interests of others." (Phil 2:2-4)

To obey this scripture we must take responsibility for the interests and needs of those around us. Over the years, I have served on more than 150 short or intermediate-term field assignments. In many of these efforts, by

Gods grace, I remembered to gauge the success of the team and the project based upon the success of each individual team member.

Everyone goes through times of weakness and struggle, especially in difficult and unknown environments such as an outreach situation. However, I cannot emphasize strongly enough that as a team you are only as strong as your weakest link. The world's system says to apply the Darwinian principle "the survival of the fittest," or the philosophy of, "Devil take the hindmost," to the weakest in our midst. Conversely, the Kingdom of God says to, "... do nothing from selfishness, ... regard one another as more important than yourselves." Just as Jesus laid down his life for us we are to lay down our lives for our friends (see John 15:13). Rather than survival of the fittest, we seek to fit all for survival.

A beneficial but challenging aspect of any difficult assignment such as an outreach, is the self-awareness that the experience can bring. Every Kingdom endeavor will produce a season of weakness for all involved: no one escapes the refining fire or the dangers of the spiritual conflict that surrounds us. However, because we have all been there (or will be) at one time or another, it is important to be aware. Take a look at things from the viewpoint of the person who is going through their "weakest link" moment.

When it is your turn to experience weakness, the big question you may find yourself asking is, "Why am I here? I don't feel useful." In that moment, it is vital to remember that God did not bring you to the field just to bench you like a third-string relief player. Therefore, if you find yourself feeling "benched" it may be that you have 'self-limited'.

Let's look some of the issues surrounding 'usability' in order to determine what will keep you off of the bench. Consider the following guidelines.

Guideline One — Stay Disciplined

"Where there is no revelation, people cast off restraint; but blessed is the one who heeds wisdom's instruction."(Prov 29:18)

Hearing the word *discipline* we often jump straight to a negative connotation. Flashbacks to childhood spankings or other forms of correction often come to mind. However, the one who is living a disciplined life does not need correction. As Proverbs instructs us, discipline is restraint. A disciplined person chooses to restrain or constrain themselves because they have revelation, or vision. Remaining disciplined in life is key to staying useful in the Kingdom.

In life there are many options. Daily, you face a tidal wave of potential distractions and stumbling blocks. The person who has vision in life and wants to be blessed will not cast off restraint. I believe the restraint mentioned in Proverbs can be understood as choosing to limit one's self - to narrow the many options of life so that you can, by wisdom's instruction, accomplish your vision.

A person living an unrestrained life is like a child in a toy store who wanders through the aisles grabbing at every colorful new toy that catches their eye. To be successful in the Kingdom enterprise that God has called you to, choose to ignore the distracting colorful options around and instead keep your eye on the prize. Remain focused and constrain your time, treasure and talent toward realizing your calling and accomplishing your vision. This is why a disciplined life style is so important: without it, you may never get out of the toy aisle of life, much less accomplish anything substantive in the Kingdom.

Guideline Two — Stay Self-Governed

"Do not be like the horse or the mule, which have no understanding but must be controlled by bit and bridle or they will not come to you." (Psalm 32:9)

Another term for self-government is self-control. For the purposes of our discussion, self-government is whether or not you will willingly submit yourself to the Lordship of Christ. The person who chooses to submit to the Lord on a daily basis is the one that God can use. If you have to have a bit and bridle put on you so that you will obey, you are considered to be a person of "no understanding."

The truth, for all mankind, is that one is never free from external authority; one only has a choice about which authority to serve. The person who resists the Lordship of Christ is trading one authority for another. For the rebel, the misguided claim is that one can be free from external authority or control, to live under one's own authority. However, as you grow in wisdom and understanding you will realize that it is not possible to live free from authority. You have to choose who will master you. The choice before you is whether to gain true freedom by choosing to submit to Christ, or to choose to live under the control of your own desires, appetites, circumstances, sin and, ultimately, yielding to the enemy of your soul. As a believer, you will discover that God, when necessary, will resort to using a "bit and bridle". This approach to discipline in your life is to draw you to him if you are not responding to his gentle, loving voice. It is not his first choice for relationship with you, but is for your own good.

God greatly prefers that you know him, trust him and willingly approach him. But if you remove yourself from under His authority, then you are resisting the protection and guidance that comes from right relationship with the Lord. Anyone who persists is resisting the Spirit of God will discover they are fending for themselves and at the mercy not only of their own devices, but also of the 'prince of the powers of the air'. It is for our own highest and best that we subject ourselves to the lover of our souls and step under the shelter of His authority. This is what we call living under the 'Lordship of Christ'. He becomes not only savior but Lord of our lives.

It is well worthwhile to evaluate whether you are choosing to be self-governed. If God has to drag you around using a bit and bridle you may not end up being his first choice for meaningful assignments. Not only does the issue of the Lordship of Christ affect your relationship with God but it will also be manifest in your relationships with your team and leaders.

There are two different types of people in Kingdom assignments. The first is the person who thinks, "I'm here. I'll do what I'm told. If God wants people to get saved or whatever, then He will bring them to me." This person is content to be externally governed, told what to do - led around by bit and bridle. These are also the people who may live through a miraculous outreach experience but only come away with memories of disappointment and frustration, or a feeling that their efforts were futile.

The second type of person draws close to the Lord. Making this choice of their own free will. From a place of deep understanding that their master is loving and trustworthy, they are always looking for his presence, and run to be close to him at every opportunity. They draw close and ask the Lord, "What should we do today? How should we do this, and, for whom should we do it?" This is the person who needs no external government or guidance by a bit and bridle. From this type of submitted and trusting relationship with God, a person finds true freedom and positions themselves for usefulness in the Kingdom.

Guideline Three — Stay healthy in soul and body

If you have not properly stewarded your soul and body you won't have much to give. God will not press you to give something that you don't have. Be good stewards of your being: body, soul and spirit.

Body Management. You limit your physical potential by your lifestyle choices. God does not hold you accountable for something you don't have, but only for what you do have. If you have some sort of limitation, whether by birth or accident, there are a number of things you may not be able to do physically or mentally. God knows that and won't expect you to climb a mountain only using your wheelchair.

However, some disciples create their own limitations through lifestyle choices. The following is a short list of culprits that dissolve our life energy and potential. Some lifestyle sins are obvious and should be addressed by each individual. In this list are items often considered less of a priority, yet they lead directly to loss of our potential :

- Laziness
- Distractions
- Overeating and poor food choices
- Lack of exercise
- Excessive gaming or TV watching
- Substance abuse and excessive use of alcohol

God wants to be the Lord of your whole being. Jesus died for all of you, not just your spirit. Of the prophesied savior Isaiah 53:5 says, "... *he was pierced for our transgressions, he was crushed for our iniquities; the punishment that brought us peace was on him, and by his wounds we are healed.*" As part of God's redemption plan there is a clear focus on healing. He is concerned about your physical well-being and the condition of your body. The main reason we often do not properly steward our physical condition is that we don't live with vision. An inspired vision will include understanding that you are important to God's plans on the earth. Therefore, if we have a proper vision of the role that God has for us in the expansion of His Kingdom, we will feel great responsibility to keep ourselves useful for that role.

Soul Management. Your soul is comprised of your Mind, Will and Emotions. Your soul and spirit are eternal and when you get to heaven, you will still think and feel and be that which makes you uniquely yourself. In addition to your spirit, God is also deeply concerned about the condition of your soul. Psalm 23:3 says, *"He restores my soul; He guides me in the paths of righteousness For His name's sake."*

You can't give out what you don't have. You may struggle with feeling underutilized during an outreach if your soul is in need of restoration. God wants to restore your soul and He is able to do just that. Signs that your soul may need restoring can be:

- Emotional neediness - lacking appropriate boundaries
- Preoccupied or negative thought patterns
- Anger issues
- Mistrust of your teammates or leaders
- Self-isolation or feeling that others are isolating you
- Self Pity
- Depression
- Bitterness and unforgiveness

These temptations often arise in an outreach context. Our souls are similar to our bodies in that they also have needs and require care to be healthy. Most of us grow up understanding that we must take care of our bodies to some extent, if we want to stay physically healthy. As believers, we also have at least a basic understanding of our spirit and its needs. Just as our physical body needs food, our spirit also needs to be fed and cared for.

The 'spirit' of a Christian is cared for primarily by the presence of God, reading the Word of God and other spiritual disciplines such as prayer and fasting. Most Christians have a general idea how to care for and steward the spirit and spiritual life. Usually these practices and understandings are based on the input from our church community and spiritual leaders.

On the other hand, the condition of one's soul is often completely neglected. God's heart and plan for you is that your soul will also prosper just as your spirit prospers in him. In the body of Christ there has been a neglect of the soul. Often, the soul is even referred to negatively as if it were somehow relegated to being a part of our original, fallen, sin nature. You might hear someone say, "that person is *soulish* or *needy*." Usually this is a negative statement in response to a person's distasteful attempts to gain affection, affirmation, comfort and acceptance.

The truth is that all of us have legitimate soul needs and God intends us to care for the soul needs of those around us. By God's original design and intention, soul needs are to be met, not only by God's gentle presence, but also by the body of Christ. After God created Adam he said, *"it is not good for man to be alone."* Therefore, He created Eve for Adam, to be a compatible companion and a, "soul-mate" for him.

In Acts 14:21-22 Paul gives a clear account of meeting the soul needs of the believers. He says, *"After they had preached the gospel to that city and had made many disciples, they returned to Lystra and to Iconium and to Antioch, strengthening the souls of the disciples, encouraging them to continue in the faith, and saying, 'Through many tribulations we must enter the kingdom of God'."* We each have a responsibility toward one another to strengthen each other's soul. This does not replace the role of God in our lives; it is God who gives us each our personal identities, but it is a God-designed role for the body of Christ that we each will be, in yet another delightful way, "my brother's keeper."

All of us go through difficult times in which our souls may struggle deeply. We may have authentic wounds from past experiences that need real healing. Through the grace of God and the blood of Jesus, healing for the soul is possible, just as much as healing for the physical body is provided for in Christ.

At times during an outreach experience God will use the context of that experience to reveal areas of your own life that need attention and healing. The downside is that if we begin to feel that we are not being useful to the team, we may begin to doubt our purpose and whether God has called us to this effort. Thoughts of self-doubt can leave you feeling paralyzed. The right response in this situation is to turn to the Lord to discover from him what he is trying to show you. He is far more concerned about the worker (you) than the work. Let Him bring healing to any wounded areas of your soul that become exposed.

Until you are healed, you are like a cracked vessel that struggles to hold any water at all, much less to have a reserve that may be poured out for others. God lets outreach experiences expose those cracks or leaks. He heals them, fills you with living water, and then guides you in pouring out the water of life. You bring healing to the nations.

Let Him heal you. Don't settle for a life defined by the unmet needs that are in your soul. If you are struggling, and find that the needs of your soul dominate your daily life, there is a secret to moving forward. The secret is to shift your eyes off of yourself and your own needs and choose to be a blessing to others. This is often how healing comes. I can guarantee that others who also are entering the Kingdom of God through many tribulations surround you. You can minister to their souls. You will find that God will meet the needs of others through you, even when you are at a weakened point in your own life. Trust Him to meet your needs and to empower you to be a blessing to those around you.

> "As He entered a village, ten leprous men who stood at a distance met Him; and they raised their voices, saying, 'Jesus, Master, have mercy on us!' When He saw them, He said to them, 'Go and show yourselves to the priests.' And as they were going, they were cleansed." (Luke 17:12-14 NASB)

There is a principle at work in this story of ten leprous men who want to be healed. Jesus told them to go *before* they were healed. In faith, they headed out to show themselves to the priests as Jesus had commanded. As they were going, they were cleansed or healed. We may find ourselves in much the same situation. God asks us to go, often long before we are fully healed.

Stepping out in obedience is an act of faith. During our 'going' we become parents, husbands, wives, workers, artists, leaders, presidents, ministers, missionaries, etc. Along the way, we realize the faithfulness of God and we can be healed of our physical afflictions and of the leprosy in our souls. As we obey and *go*, we are healed.

Another beautiful aspect of this story is found in Luke 17:15-19, "*Now one of them, when he saw that he had been healed, turned back, glorifying God with a loud voice, and he fell on his face at His feet, giving thanks to Him. And he was a Samaritan. Then Jesus answered and said, 'Were there not ten cleansed? But the nine — where are they? Was no one found who returned to give glory to God, except this foreigner?' And He said to him, 'Stand up and go; your faith has made you well.'"*

The one leper got more than the other nine who were also physically healed. This leper is the one whose heart was bound to the healer through the experience of being physically healed. He returned and passionately glorified, thanked and worshiped Jesus. That leper is an example of the one who does not need the bit and bridle to draw him to the master. He willingly and zealously responded to the tug on his heart to return and worship the Lord. In so doing, this healed leper received even more blessing.

In Christ's last statement in this passage, he said, "Stand up and go; your faith has made you *well.*" The word "well" in the original text is, "Sozo". That word means more than healed, it means, "whole." This man was healed physically like the other lepers but he was also restored or healed in his soul. Many are healed but not all are made whole. God desires to heal your body and to heal the leprosy in your soul. Those that willingly come and submit to the Lordship of Christ are made whole.

Chapter 9
The Pursuit of Romance

"... let us run with endurance the race that is set before us, fixing our eyes on Jesus, the author and perfecter of faith ... "(Heb 12:1b-2a)

IN MANY OUTREACHES I HAVE OBSERVED NO greater threat to the success of the overall effort than unmanaged romantic inclinations. Don't get me wrong, there is nothing wrong with being attracted to someone during your field assignment, but there are risks to these attractions that can be minimized by the application of wisdom and experience.

If you are single, managing your romantic interests will be one of your greatest challenges while completing your field assignment. You will discover that there are amazing, like-minded and attractive individuals working alongside you on your team. You would be hard-pressed to find higher quality candidates who could become your spouse one day. However, the challenge here is the context and timing.

Remember, you have been assigned a race. If you are serving in a short-term project, you are essentially running a spiritual sprint. Jesus would not have called you into your assignment unless he knew you had something to offer on the field. It is up to you to keep your eyes fixed on Jesus and, in partnership with him, to bring a blessing to the place where you are serving.

The primary, problematic dynamic is that you are serving in a high-stress context that is far outside of your usual realm of life experience. In a context like this, you will find that you are exceedingly vulnerable to influences in your environment, to other individuals, and even to your own soul needs. You may find that your natural response to an insecure environment is to seek security. A season of intense difficulty and pain may cause alterations to your emotional life that will move you toward seeking comfort at all cost.

While this is a normal part of human nature, it must be managed. You cannot let your emotions and needs govern you: you must master them. When you allow Him to do so, God will use these circumstances to build your strength so that you will be in authority over your environment and your environment will not overcome you. The person who overcomes is able to manage the demands of their own soul and is one step closer to long-term spiritual strength.

I was 19 years old when I first observed what can happen at the intersection of outreach and romance. During this particular three month outreach to Ukraine one of the staff members for my student team was a young man about 25 years old. During the field assignment it became easy to see that he was strongly attracted to a female student on our team. Right from the beginning we noticed an immediate fascination between them and they made little effort to manage their interest in each other, despite a, "no dating" policy in the program.

This was a particularly difficult outreach both physically and spiritually, and because these two individuals allowed their need for emotional support and comfort to guide their decision-making, they became a committed couple during the trip. This outreach required all of us to persevere through incredibly difficult challenges. Team members who had decided not to pursue any romantic interests during the program were doing their best to intensely pursue their relationship with Jesus, and were learning how to let Jesus meet their emotional needs. Nevertheless, this romantic relationship in our midst produced a level of friction and even envy toward our team-mates who were obviously focusing their emotions on one another and supporting each other at the expense of team unity.

The problem was that their 'love' was not real. Even though they had become serious about each other to the point of looking at engagement rings, the relationship was artificial. It was based on mutual need for comfort and support during a difficult time and was not based on true love.

True love means doing what is highest and best for another person at any given time. When romantic relationships form in the context of duress or hardship, often the basis for the relationship is an attempt by each individual to meet a certain needs of their own. The basis of a *healthy* relationship is that each individual has decided to serve the other person, and to pour love, encouragement, help, and effort into the life of the other person. When the people involved in a relationship are focused on what they can get from it, instead of what they can give, this is a clear indicator that the roots of that relationship are unhealthy.

The couple on my outreach learned the hard way about the pitfalls of forming a romantic relationship while in the midst of a challenging outreach. When they returned home the girl simply disappeared out of the guy's life. He was devastated. Once she returned to her customary environment, this young woman realized that the entire context of their relationship was flawed: it had been a coping mechanism, and once there was nothing difficult left to cope with, the relationship fell apart. This couple had been living in a fantasy of their own making. Their relationship was formed in a context that was not going to continue in the normal world. Having had this revelation, she broke off the relationship within a couple of days of returning home.

Under the circumstances, breaking up was the right thing to do. But the saddest part of this was that they had both missed out on a once-in-a-lifetime opportunity to really bond with their other teammates while on outreach, and also to allow the Lord the opportunity to truly meet their needs during a hard experience. Correspondingly, the team had suffered from the loss of the contributions these two could have made had they not been otherwise occupied. The team also experienced an actual negative impact because of their impractical romantic relationship. It was truly a loss for all involved.

My exhortation to those who find themselves in any similar situation, is to take the opportunity to go deeper in relationship with the Lord in a whole new way. If you go into a relationship in a needy and broken condition, you will inevitably suck the life out of the person who is the object of your affection. Let God heal you and be your source in life. He wants to fill you up so you can find a spouse and have a meaningful, life-long relationship that arises from an overflow of His love and power inside you.

If you allow God to be in control of your romantic inclinations he will bring the right person alongside you during the right time in your race (Hebrews 12:1). The person he brings alongside of you won't cause you to drop out of the race that is set before you. You will find that in God's design, the person you fall in love with will be able to run the race with you, even speeding you towards the, "upward call of Christ."

Philippians 3:14 says, *"I press on toward the goal for the prize of the upward call of God in Christ Jesus."* If you allow God to design your romantic pursuit, you and your spouse will be able to press on together toward the prize, the upward call of God!

Here are a few important principles that I consider vital for success when outreach and romance cross paths.

1 — Build relationships wisely. Be cautious about forming romantic relationships when you are in an environment that is:

1. Unpredictable
2. Full of the unknown or unfamiliar
3. Stressful or full of physical hardship
4. Filled with emotional pain

Pursuing a relationship in these unusual contexts could produce something that is artificial and unsustainable. God wants you and the object of your romantic interest to be blessed, but if you are building a relationship on unstable ground it will lead to a collapse.

2 — Seek counsel for exceptions. Someone might argue an exception — that one who is abandoned to, and committed to, following God wherever He may lead is living an inherently unpredictable life; and that God does sometimes choose to bring us to our spouses in the midst of unusual circumstances. In such a situation wisdom, discernment, and wise counsel are called for. However, if the potential for a marriage relationship is truly from the Lord, there is no rush. Relax, and trust that the Lord will work it all out after your short-term outreach concludes.

3 — Form relationships while you are in a place of wholeness and strength. This will give you the ability to lay a good foundation for your relationship and your motivation can remain pure. If you form a romantic relationship while in a place of weakness or neediness, your motive, though unintentional, could either be to have your emotional needs met, or to get something from the other person that you feel will bring life to your soul. While recognizing that none of us are ever completely whole and perfect on this side of heaven, nevertheless it is best to form relationships from a motive that is all about doing what is highest and best for the other person. This is the definition of true love; doing what is highest and best for another. This kind of love, along with the wholeness of our souls, can only come from Christ.

4 — Don't take advantage of another person's vulnerabilities. These can be caused by the intense and difficult nature of a short-term outreach environment: the temptation is to displace God in another person's life by becoming their comfort and salvation. When God intentionally brings us into and through these very difficult times, his goal is for us to draw near to him, learn to trust him, and learn to let him meet all of our needs. If you interject yourself as another person's savior or comforter during this process, you run the risk of becoming an idol. God will jealously guard his position in our lives; so don't set yourself up as an idol in someone else's life, especially when they are in a place of vulnerability.

5 — Avoid emotional idolatry. When in a painful or needy situation, our natural response is to look for a way to escape or to cope. In my experience, the strongest temptation is to look to another person to provide emotional or physical comfort as we attempt to flee the pain caused by our situation. This is a wrong motivation for pursuing a relationship and will lead to emotional escapism. This type of escapism can produce deep and unhealthy emotional bonding with the person we use only as a coping mechanism. In truth, this is a form of idolatry. If you do not give in to escapism you will overcome. God wants you to bond with him emotionally before you attempt to bond with another person.

"*And if one can overpower him who is alone, two can resist him. A cord of three strands is not quickly torn apart.*"(Eccl 4:9) God wants to be the second strand in your life so that you can resist the devil who seeks to overpower you. The third strand is your spouse. It is God's design that your relationship will be strong and not easily torn apart… but you must have the correct *second strand* in your life to truly have a strong, life-long relationship with another person.

6 — Choose to bond with your team as a family. "*Do not rebuke an older man harshly, but exhort him as if he were your father. Treat younger men as brothers, older women as mothers, and younger women as sisters, with absolute purity.*"(1 Tim 5:1-2) Here scripture gives us a clear instruction about how we should treat the family of God around us. If you want to have an effective outreach and create friends for life, then it is wise to obey this scripture.

7 — Treat others as brothers and sisters in Christ. Guys (and girls), treat women as sisters… with absolute purity! Girls (and guys), treat men as your brothers. Using this model of relationship in your team, you will create an atmosphere of purity and freedom that will produce incredible joy. During a difficult and compressed experience, just choose to be brothers and sisters. Let God be God in other people by choosing to add value to those around you instead of trying to get something from them in order to meet your own need.

8 — Avoid a very expensive date. The Lord has sent you into this assignment because he knows you and knows what is best for you. He may want to move powerfully through you during this experience or he may want to put you in a position where you will have a chance to grow. Probably, you will find yourself in both of these situations during your outreach.

What God did *not* intend to do was to send you on a very expensive date. If you go into an assignment with this in mind it will keep the *main thing* (reaching the lost) as the *main thing*. God can arrange much cheaper dating options when you get back home! This is a perfect time to demonstrate good stewardship over the resources that God provided to enable you to participate in your project or outreach.

> *"After a long time the master of those servants returned and settled accounts with them. The man who had received five bags of gold brought the other five. 'Master,' he said, 'you entrusted me with five bags of gold. See, I have gained five more. His master replied, 'Well done, good and faithful servant! You have been faithful with a few things; I will put you in charge of many things. Come and share your master's happiness!'"* (Matt 25:19-21)

If you treat this assignment as a thing of great worth that God has entrusted to you, you will have a chance to bring joy to him by proving to be a wise and trustworthy steward. God wants you to learn to be faithful with the few things so that He can entrust you with much. We all want to hear the Lord say, "Well done, good and faithful servant!"

Chapter 10
The Alien Mind

DEEP IN THE CENTER OF INDIA THERE is a small town with a population of 100,000 residents: small by Indian standards, but large enough to get lost in for a few hours. Our team arrived early in the day. We had just completed a four-hour drive though dusty jungle roads. Throngs of people came out to see the strange group of foreigners. Small children began to grab our arms and tried desperately to rub the white off of our hands and arms. They were convinced that we were really dark skinned like them, but that we had some kind of paint or coating on our skin that made us appear white! They had never seen a foreigner before, and they had rarely seen other Indians from outside of their region.

We traveled with six local pastors and missionaries, and our project was to set up a temporary dental clinic in this small town. We aimed to provide free dental care for as many local people as possible before leaving in the evening. An experienced American dentist was with us. He had completed dozens of such outreaches and had once extracted over 72 teeth in a single day. To fix bad cavities in the usual, western sense, was not possible in these contexts, so all he could offer the people was relief from pain by safely and painlessly extracting the problem teeth.

During outreaches in other villages, some of our team members served as volunteer assistants to this dentist, while the rest of our team conducted worship services, offered healing prayer, and shared our faith with the hundreds of people waiting for dental care. This had proved to be a very effective model, and because we provided very real and needed services to the local population, the local officials were tolerant of our sharing about Christ in the process.

In this particular town, our first stop was to visit the only known Christian in the entire area. We visited his small home and ate a delicious meal of homemade local dishes. Our host began to explain to us that this town was a center for radical Hinduism and their sacrificial rituals. This had prevented a Christian presence or outreach in this region at any time in history.

He went on to explain how once a year, hundreds of thousands of people converged on this town and its prominent Hindu temple complex. Their purpose was to sacrifice 100,000 animals as a form of worship to their temple gods. The particular Hindu deity that was worshiped and revered in the massive local temple complex was the goddess of death, Kali. In this one gruesome day each year, these 100,000 animals were slaughtered, and their blood spread over every building in the city. The locals told us that the blood ran deep in the streets during the ceremony. This was serious spiritual business, and the massive temple that stood overlooking the city was the guardian of all of Kali's interests.

In this particular town, shortly after arriving, word reached us from the Hindu priests and local officials that we would not be allowed to conduct our dental clinic or share publicly. This news came as no real surprise to us as we had begun to learn about the intensely controlled spiritual environment in this place. We also received a warning through some local people that the Hindu militant groups in town had threatened our safety unless we left town within a couple of hours. These threats were not idle, and I had been in close proximity to many riots and attacks in this part of India. Several of my Indian pastor friends and their church members had been beaten severely on multiple occasions. A revered American missionary and his children had recently been killed in this area.

We prayed with the local believer who had hosted us, and then decided to retreat to the outer edge of the town. The local authorities had not said that we could not set up our clinic outside of the town boundaries, so we proceeded to live by the letter of the law, and set up our dental clinic just outside the last area of homes. Ironically, this placed us near to the massive, arching gateway that led into the temple of Kali.

While most of the team prepared for the clinic and the upcoming programs, three of us decided we were going to walk up to the temple to discover first-hand what was going on in this hostile and highly spiritual environment. During my ministry I learned that if one was not acting in a hostile or offensive manner (truly moving in the opposite spirit) one would generally be well received by temple priests and officials. After praying, we felt that God wanted us to go and visit this Hindu site, so we hiked up the steep path to the massive structure above us.

When we arrived at the temple complex, I thought we had stepped from reality into an Indiana Jones-type action movie. There were ceremonies and chanting going on all around us while priests garbed in wildly colorful robes moved throughout the complex attending to their rituals. We walked past a large room with an open front. Inside there was a massive statue of the Hindu deity, Kali, who ruled this temple and this region.

As we proceeded through the complex we arrived at the central courtyard. Evenly spaced in the courtyard were the twenty-foot wide openings to four wells. Before we could get close enough to see how deep were the wells, three priests armed with swords confronted us. As they stepped in front of us to block our path, my heightened spiritual senses told me that we were actually being confronted by the spiritual powers that claimed ownership of this area.

One of the priests, hand still on the hilt of his sword, began to speak in perfect English. He said, "Do you see these wells? Once a year, when we conduct our sacrifices, our gods come and fill these wells with pure butter. We sell the butter and the whole town lives off of the income for an entire year. What can your god do?" The challenge in his voice was searing and hateful. This thinly veiled challenge to the one true God had been thrown at us.

Suddenly, we found ourselves in a situation not very different from events the prophet Elijah faced when he confronted the prophets of Baal. The Old Testament book of 1st Kings and Chapter 18 tells the story. As I faced these priests who were spiritually charged for a physical confrontation, I was listening to the Lord for direction. In my own heart, I thought this kind of spiritual confrontation, or power encounter, could play out in a very interesting way! However, as I tuned into the heart of the Lord, I felt a very different sense of direction.

Even though these priests were ready and willing to either kill us or attempt to overcome us spiritually, in that moment I sensed a strong love and compassion from the Lord for them. One of the keys to successful spiritual warfare is to move in the opposite spirit. If someone comes against you in hate then you reach out in love. This opposite reaction will literally defuse both spiritually and naturally volatile situations.

So, as the priests waited for my response to their challenge of, "What can your god do?" I just smiled at them and said, "Oh, that's nice," and introduced myself. I began asking them who they were and what their names were. They were totally caught off guard as they, and the spirits inside them, had tried their best scare tactic on us and it hadn't affected us. Instead, we asked them to show us around the facility. Totally deflated by the lack of response to their challenge, they agreed to give us a tour of the temple.

With hands still on their swords, they proceeded to boastfully show us the wonders of the temple, and the statue of their greatest deity, Kali, the goddess of death. After a short tour we decided that it was wise to make our way back to the edge of the town and rejoin our medical team. By God's overcoming grace, we saw dozens of people relieved from their physical pain. Many found Christ that day and were relieved of their spiritual suffering as well. All in all, it was a good day on the field of outreach.

Consider with me some of the ways Scripture teaches us about this conflict of kingdoms.

—— * ——

"For consider Him who endured such hostility from sinners against Himself, lest you become weary and discouraged in your souls." (Heb 12:3)

When you set out to represent the Kingdom of God you will sometimes encounter unreasonable, even irrational, hostility and resistance. These are focused at your spirit, your health, your thoughts and emotions. For those who are under the control of the evil one, it is the natural thing to do. This should come as no surprise. What really matters, though, is how you respond in these situations. Remember, Jesus endured great hostility against himself from sinners.

The scriptures exhort us to keep this in mind. As we encounter this hostility and spiritual warfare it can produce weariness and discouragement. The key to navigating in the rough waters where two spiritual kingdoms are colliding is to know that you have an, *Alien* mind. You may not now know this, but you are truly an Alien to the world's system.

—— * ——

"If you belonged to the world, it would love you as its own. As it is, you do not belong to the world, but I have chosen you out of the world. That is why the world hates you." (John 15:19)

Jesus said that because of the Holy Spirit of God, and the seed of eternal life living within you, you are, literally, no longer "of the world" and, "the world hates you." It seems inexplicable when the unseen force Jesus called "the world" rises up against your for no apparent reason.

Just as with the Hindu priests who confronted us, the world's agents and representatives will be quick to identify you as, "being from another Kingdom," and you will be seen as a threat by the, "prince of the power of the air."

—— * ——

"For He rescued us from the domain of darkness, and transferred us to the kingdom of His beloved Son, in whom we have redemption, the forgiveness of sins." (Colossians 1:13)

Once you are justified in Christ, free from your trespasses and sins, you have switched Kingdoms and Christ is at work in you.

—— * ——

"You were dead in your trespasses and sins, in which you formerly walked according to the course of this world, according to the prince of the power of the air, of the spirit that is now working in the sons of disobedience." (Ephesians 2:1-2)

The "sons of disobedience," mentioned in this scripture, are manipulated against you by the one who is at work in them. Your own alien status in this world will make you a target of hostility.

One thing about being alien in this world is that you can see things differently. You have alien eyesight that sees things for what they really are and not what the world's darkness says things are. The secret to overcoming in any situation is to be able to see what is really going on through spiritual eyes. You have to keep your alien eyesight engaged!

—— * ——

"So we fix our eyes not on what is seen, but on what is unseen, since what is seen is temporary, but what is unseen is eternal." (2 Cor 4:18)

In this conflict of kingdoms, your enemy wants you to react to his efforts according to the same spirit he is using to attack you. In these difficult conflicts, if he can get you to align with his methods, you have functionally submitted yourself to the enemy of your soul. At this point, instead of serving the purposes of the Kingdom of God you will find yourself unintentionally reinforcing the enemy's efforts and claims instead of opposing him. This is why it's so important to move in the opposite spirit.

How do we avoid this catastrophic possibility? We have to keep our discernment or, *spiritual eyesight*, engaged at all times. 2 Corinthians 4:18 clearly says that, "we look not at the things which are seen, but at the things which are not seen." It is important to discipline yourself to look through a natural situation, in order to see what is spiritually happening behind the scenes. I was able to respond in the right way to these violently confrontational Hindu priests because I looked through them to see that they were literally pawns of the enemy controlled through deception and sin. They needed someone to show them unconditional love and to value them as people.

At that time, they did not need to be confronted by an Elijah. By recognizing the spiritual power that enabled their behavior I was able to look at them as persons loved of God. I then was able to receive God's heart of love for them. I was able to change my own reactions to the confrontation, toward the evil spirits who were at work in them, rather than reacting against them as individuals. People are God's precious creations and are to be valued above all else. Using my alien eyesight allows me to focus on the things which are not seen. This is how you love the unlovable. This is how you overcome and walk in the correct attitude of mind and heart — that which is characterized by the Holy Spirit himself.

— * —

"Set your mind on the things above, not on the things that are on earth." (Col 3:2)

If your mind is set on the things of earth you will be buffeted and crushed by the world system around you. By setting your mind on the things above you can live heavenly-minded even in the darkest pits of hell. You can do it with unconditional love and joy in your heart.

Here are just a few of the tests that may come your way while you are involved in an outreach situation. I call these the, "Earthly Minded Tests." Your response to these and other similar situations will expose whether or not you are setting your mind on things above and seeing with your alien perspective.

- Taxi Drivers in General
- Bargaining
- Theft and Getting Ripped-Off (especially a challenge for the guys)
- Harassment (especially a challenge for the girls)
- Wrongful treatment of the women on your team by local men
- Criticism of your home country or culture
- Rejection of the Gospel
- Rejection or discrimination against you or others from your team
- Persecution
- Cultural Frustrations
- Weariness and Loneliness
- Corruption and Corrupt Authorities
- Violence directed at you or your team
- Discord or strife within your team or field partners

Keep your heart right. To keep your heart right is the highest form of victory in any outreach context. Maintaining a heart of love toward the nationals where you are working, as well as toward the members of your team, is a true outreach victory. This list of a few generalized, principled responses to these kinds of tests will help you align with God's heart for the people and place in which you are working.

- It's better to get ripped-off and still be able to be a witness, rather than to fight for your 'rights' and make enemies of the Gospel
- Don't fight *the system* in your location because you won't win and you'll end up living in frustration
- Learn to use the existing systems and structures as righteously as possible
- Keep a good sense of humor about everything
- Don't give in to mockery or a negative attitude about the people, culture or place
- Don't make degrading comments about a country's situation: it's offensive, hurtful and prideful
- Don't make jokes about a country, culture or the problems you perceive; the locals are well aware of their problems and don't need you to remind them
- Avoid comparing your home country with your outreach location, both in your heart and aloud

- Seek to empathize with and understand the cultures and peoples with whom you interact
- Keep the attitude of a learner
- Keep a servant heart and interact with people as Jesus did

How can you tell if you have been *earthly minded* in any of these areas? Ask yourself this question. Following this encounter, could I share the gospel in love and sincerity with this person or people? If you cannot honestly say "Yes", then you will know that you have failed to keep love in the forefront and to keep your mind set on things above.

These lists of problems and their heart-attitude solutions are not exhaustive. There are many and varied issues you will face on outreach, however, the principles outlined here are broad enough to be applied in most situations.

Remember, your own personal victory is not determined by checking off the box marked, "How many people got saved?" but instead, by what process you have used to achieve these Kingdom results.

Chapter 11
You Smell

When I was working in the former Soviet Union in the early 1990's, it was an era before deodorant had made its way into the popular culture of the region. One particular experience pushed me to the edge of my tolerance for physical discomfort. We were a team of 14 working in Ukraine during the summer of 1993. Each day we traveled to multiple ministry sites. Sometimes by local bus, often on foot because the buses failed to run, or were too full of people. One particular bus trip stands out in my memory. Those two hours are among the most agonizing of my life. We were used to crowded and hot conditions, but the dynamics of this particular ride were entirely another level of challenge.

As usual, we had packed the entire team onto an already overcrowded bus. Since I was one of the bigger guys on the team, my job was to bring up the rear of our group as we wrangled our way into the bus. I shoved our people through the automatic doors while holding on to the entry rail bars. I felt like Hercules or Sampson as I used all of my strength to push our team far enough into the bus so that the door could close behind me. For the rest of the ride I was smashed against the door. To say it was an unpleasant part of our daily routine is an understatement.

This particular ride was unique because of the sizable group of little, aged Ukrainian ladies on board this bus. They were the meanest and feistiest group of elderly people you could ever come across. One of the superstitions prevalent among this older generation was that anyone who encountered a breeze, or airflow in general, would get the flu. Despite the fact that it was more 90 degrees outside, and that inside the bus the temperature was above 110 degrees, the little old ladies would not tolerate even a slightly cracked-open window! With no air movement and no air-conditioning on the bus, the heat and bodies began to produce an overwhelming aroma.

There were more than 100 people crowded into a bus that was designed to seat 50 and allow for another 40 to stand. The bus was so heavy that our back bumper was nearly dragging on the ground. When the smell of body odor became so incredibly strong as to overwhelm a local Ukrainian, he attempted to pop open a roof-top vent for relief.

However, the little old ladies would have none of it, and formed the elderly equivalent of an armored battle line. They began shouting and stabbing with their canes and umbrellas. The air-flow-violator was jabbed and beaten into submission, and the vents were closed once again. With eyes watering from the acrid, ammonia smell, we persevered through the trip.

Have you ever been around someone who has neglected to wear deodorant in really hot weather? Or, have you ever been around someone who has put on over-loads of perfume? These scenarios produce a very real and distinctive reaction in those who are nearby. What you discover when you enter the Kingdom of God is that you have a particular *spiritual aroma*, and the spiritual aromas that characterize various spiritual pursuits are each unique and distinctive. It actually depends upon which kingdom a person is aligned with.

The sweet aroma that we carry is the fragrance of Christ.

"But thanks be to God, who always leads us in triumph in Christ, and manifests through us the sweet aroma of the knowledge of Him in every place. For we are a fragrance of Christ to God among those who are being saved and among those who are perishing; to the one an aroma from death to death, to the other an aroma from life to life ... "(2 Cor 2:14-16)

India is never a predictable place and has never failed to amaze me. During one particular season of ministry, our team was partnering with a local Church-planting ministry in India. In our four-wheel drive vehicle we traveled to a couple villages each day. This area of India was incredibly remote. Most of the villages had never seen foreigners, and none of them had ever been given an opportunity to hear the Gospel or to experience the physical and spiritual healing that comes through the name of Jesus. These villages were either very interested and wanted to hear about the message of Christ, or they were outright hostile and at times dangerous.

One particular night on this trip brought me to a deeper understanding of 2 Corinthians 2:14-16. The Apostle Paul wrote this letter to the first century Corinthian church. He too, was familiar with sharing the Gospel in hostile environments. Think about the aroma he referring to. To some people witnessing Christians are the aroma of "Death to Death" and to others we are the aroma of "Life to Life."

To those who are being saved, believing, witnessing Christians are a wonderful, fragrant aroma that reminds them of Jesus. But to those who have rejected Christ or are outside of his Kingdom, that same aroma becomes the smell of death. Is it the aroma of their own death? It seems that this death-to-death aroma experience is at a deep spiritual level in a non-believer, beyond rational understanding.

It is not that you smell like a dead mouse, in the natural sense. The spirit of a person under the control of the evil one is reminded of their own lost, eternal condition by the fragrance of heaven that you carry in the spiritual realm. Awareness in the spirit of separation from God, death and bondage are stirred up by the aroma of Christ in both the individual who is not yet redeemed and the powers of darkness that have gained access in their lives. When a person is being saved, the aroma of Christ reminds them that they have been made alive in Christ and are now in the Kingdom of God.

"He has rescued us from the power of darkness and transferred us into the kingdom of his beloved Son"(Col 1:13 NKJV)

This reality is why you, as a believer, may encounter so many strange and inexplicable reactions to the aroma of heavenly life that you carry and the message of Christ that you represent.

The negative unprovoked reactions, emotions and responses that someone manifests toward you, may well be the expression of the demonic entities that can bind an unbeliever.

Many Christians believe these expressions of demonic displeasure can be identified as *demonic manifestations*. The devil hates Christ, hates you, and hates that you are moving from life to life. He also hates that he and his servants are inescapably moving from death to death. With them there is no possibility of redemption. Your life giving Christian aroma reminds him that he lost the war and the Kingdom of God was established when God raised Jesus from the dead.

The aroma of Christ that emanates from your redeemed and sanctified spirit reminds Satan of his fate and threatens the last vestige of his control over the world. The aroma of your life and witness diminishes Satan's ability to coerce humans to align their wills with his. You smell! …And your smell is going to get a reaction!

Meanwhile, back to the story about India…

This particular evening event seemed like it was going well right from the start. After three hours of very challenging off-road driving, our team arrived at a remote village in central India around 6:00 PM We joined our Indian host pastor and his church-planting team. The village was largely comprised of tiny, round, mud huts that were no more than 5 feet tall. We left our jeeps at the far end of the village where the road ended and made our way through the village and entered the courtyard of the village leader's house.

At night, the only light in the entire village came from a single large light bulb that was connected to long, wires that had been thrown over the high-voltage power lines running above the village. It was a dangerous arrangement. Sadly, we discovered that two men had been electrocuted during their attempts to hijack that electricity. They just want a single light bulb for their village.

We sat on a ground cloth, situated with our backs toward the village leader's larger, adobe style house. On two sides of his courtyard stood long adobe walls pointing away from the house. A massive bonfire had been lit in the courtyard fire pit, and hundreds of villagers had gathered to hear the message we had to share. They were seated directly across the fire pit from us. The bonfire brilliantly lighted the crowd.

When we arrived a young, well-dressed Indian man, who had returned to his village after studying at university, met us. He spoke perfect English and we initially assumed that he was favorably disposed toward us. He had been very welcoming and talkative. As our Indian pastor friends began to introduce us, and then to introduce the Gospel to the villagers, I noticed that not all was well. The university man was sitting in the fourth row of villagers just beyond the bonfire, and he was becoming quite agitated. He began jerking and twitching as we continued to share testimonies of God's love and work in our lives.

As we began handing out large numbers of Bibles, this young man was overcome by demons. As the Bibles were handed back through the crowd, he jumped to his feet and began screaming. He had a Bible in hand, lit it on fire, and hurled it toward our team! Then this bizarre behavior began to spread like a virus in a zombie movie. Similar expressions of rage and other erratic behavior spread through the crowd. A full-blown riot had erupted and now it was time to go.

The Indian pastor and I quickly gathered our team, and I yelled for them to run to the jeeps! As we made a quick exit out the side of the courtyard, the crowd that had become a mob pursued us. We had a vague sense of where we had left the jeeps but the single village light bulb had gone out and it was completely dark. Still we ran.

As we ran two things began to happen. First, we didn't remember the clothes lines strung up for drying laundry. I could hear loud thumps and groans as people were knocked off their feet by the clothes lines strung from hut to hut. There was something very funny about this and as we began to laugh out load as we ran. Then we saw that the sky was filled with small balls of fire that began to rain down on us. We realized these balls of fire were Bibles lighted on fire and thrown at us by the pursuing mob!

The Indian pastor running alongside me began to laughingly yell out the scripture from Psalm 119:105, *"Your word is a lamp to my feet and a light to my path!"* Rocks and flaming Bibles were landing all around us and bouncing off of our vehicles as we speedily loaded up and drove away! The next day, the village elders sent a letter of apology to the Indian pastors and invited them to come again. The very next evening they returned and were able to share the gospel with no further riots or flaming bibles. Half of the village received Christ and two churches were planted. God can redeem all things!

This situation was a clear example of the aroma of Christ setting off a negative spiritual reaction. There had been no reason for such a violent reaction to our interaction with the villagers. The village leaders themselves had invited us. The enemy had responded aggressively through the well-dressed college student, and he instigated a riot to frustrate the sharing of the message of the cross.

Earlier in my career a similar situation occurred in Ukraine. This was my first experience with overt spiritual hostility. It was also an experience that taught me the true power that is found in the name of Jesus.

Our team had planned an evangelistic event that day, but it rained. We found ourselves huddled under the overhanging front porch of the beautiful ballet theater located in the heart of the city. A deluge of rain had moved in and we were not prepared with umbrellas or raincoats so we took shelter under the porch roof of the theater. The theater was situated at the center of a massive plaza, probably the size of a football field. After an hour of cold rain we began to be really bored. Quietly, our team began to sing some worship songs together and to pray blessings out over the city. To our knowledge, we were the very first Christian team to ever work openly in this city. Ukraine had only been open to foreigners for a couple of years. There were only a couple of known churches in the city and they had both been formed less than six months ago. This was brand new terrain, and wide open for the Kingdom of God. During our previous two months in the region, through our evangelism and healing ministries, we had seen nearly 1000 people per day coming to the Lord. We felt privileged and honored to conduct these ministries.

Eventually we noticed two elderly ladies, dressed in black. They were only about five feet tall and had just appeared out of the rainstorm. Within seconds, they had begun yelling at us and waving their umbrellas toward us in an angry manner. With no regard for the rain they continued their verbal assault. Our team leader and his wife, who spoke Ukrainian, tried to speak peaceably with these women but this only inflamed them. As if out of nowhere, more people began to appear out of the rain from what had been empty space just moments before.

They joined the old ladies and began to angrily shout at us! Within a few minutes, a crowd of three hundred people had rallied out of nowhere and formed a half-circle around the porch where we had sought shelter from the rain.

This was my first experience with becoming the target of a full-blown riot. There was no reasoning with the crowd as they continued to shout, yell, and wave umbrellas in our direction. What had begun with our team quietly praying had now turned into a very dangerous situation.

I looked around at my team members as we slowly retreated until our backs were against the locked front doors of the theater. Panic had set in and the team was beginning to give in to fear, and not without just cause. I sensed that this crowd was about to rush in and attack us at any moment. Our team leaders continued their attempt to reason with the crowd, but our team members began to move out in all directions. Their obvious intention was to make a run for it. Suddenly, I had an overwhelming urge to intervene by rallying my teammates to pray. "Oh, no you don't!" I said to them. As they started to scatter I reached out to grab those nearest to me, dragging them together into a circle, and commanded them to pray. A few of them reluctantly began to pray aloud, but the sound of their prayers was shouted down by the crowd. In my spirit I heard the Lord say, "You command this crowd." Obediently, and without much consideration, I stepped forward and raised my hands up over the crowd and said, "In the name of Jesus, I command peace over this crowd!" Almost instantly, the near-riot quieted and the crowd went silent.

What a lesson in the power that is available to those who are in Christ Jesus! Our team leaders instantly recognized this moment of opportunity and they began speaking to the now-receptive crowd. Within a few minutes we had gone from a potentially life-threatening riot, to an open-air evangelism event! By the time our team leader finished sharing and inviting the people to respond to Jesus, more than thirty of the former rioters accepted Christ on the spot! Unfortunately, the little old ladies that the enemy used to instigate the whole event did not respond and departed, still angry against us.

You may not set off any riots by carrying the aroma of Christ, but you will surely find yourself in situations where a negative or deceitful reaction against you makes no sense.

The purpose of sharing these stories with you is to illustrate that there is a lot more going on in the unseen realm than what you can see in the natural. You have to keep a spiritual perspective if you are going to navigate the ever-expanding Kingdom of God, and overcome in every situation. If you take things at face-value in the natural, you will be tempted to become offended and hardened against the very people that God has sent you to love.

Chapter 12

The Arrow of Offense

IN GREEK MYTHOLOGY, ACHILLES WAS THE HERO of the Trojan War. He was the central character and the greatest warrior of Homer's *Iliad*. Although the death of Achilles is not presented in the Iliad, other sources concur that Paris, who shot him in the heel with a poisoned arrow, killed him near the end of the Trojan War. Later legends state that Achilles' body was invulnerable, except for his heel. Because of his death from a small wound in his heel, the term "Achilles' Heel" has come to mean a person's point of weakness.

Like this description of Achilles from Greek mythology, believers can also have a point of extreme vulnerability. No matter how strong we are in the Lord or how mature we may be in our spiritual walk, it is possible for Christians to have a similar vulnerability. It is a place in your heart that, if struck by the poisonous arrow of offense, it will at the least immobilize you, and at worst destroy you.

I have seen the damage that this arrow has caused, not only among new believers but also among the more senior figures in the body of Christ. Everyone can face a situation where arrows of offense are speeding towards this place of spiritual and emotional vulnerability. Of all the types of arrows that will be fired at you during the course of your life, none are more prevalent than the one that, once lodged in your Achilles' Heel, causes you to take on offense toward another person.

The odd part of this scenario is that, although we have a choice about whether or not this arrow will be allowed to poison us once it strikes, often we offer no resistance.

The Bible says in Proverbs 19:11, "A person's wisdom yields patience; it is to one's glory to overlook an offense.'"

The simple way to defend against this potential injury is to simply overlook the offense. The idea is to just look past it; look past what has been said or what has been done. Even though you may feel you have a legitimate reason to take up an offense, if you do, you will not only bring destruction on yourself, but you will also miss out on a chance to gain glory from heaven!

> *"We all, with unveiled face, beholding as in a mirror the glory of the Lord, are being transformed into the same image from glory to glory, just as from the Lord, the Spirit."* (2 Cor 3:18)

The idea of becoming glorious is to become more like the author of glory. The more like Jesus we become, the more glorious we become. Overlooking an offense is a central dynamic of being transformed into the likeness of Christ.

The fact that we can defend our vulnerability by simply looking past, or overlooking, offenses, is obvious. Think about it like this. We are rarely offended by the words or conduct of people who we expect to be offensive. The behavior of unreached peoples who become spiritually stirred up against us and then verbally or physically abuse us, is a good example of this idea.

When working in Brazil with a large team of young missionaries, we often conducted street performances and shared the gospel in city squares and public places. One person who lived on the streets often attended our performances, only to vent his hostility toward us and rail against the message. This man was oppressed and controlled by the enemy. He endeavored to distract people from listening to us by the most extreme behavior. Often he ran naked through the middle of our street performance, kicking over our performance props and screaming! We just ignored his bizarre behavior. Then he would then go through the crowd, overtly trying to steal their wallets and purses in order to spark a violent and distracting response. Often it worked! We decided to station team members inside the crowds who attended our events, to watch for this man's approach.

We realized that he was terribly oppressed by the devil and needed deliverance. When the spotters for our team saw him coming from one direction or another, he was usually naked, screaming, and waving his arms in the air as he ran toward us. Our team members began to raise their hands and pray against the spirit who was at work in the man, and when they did this, he would veer off and run screaming in another direction. We realized that praying against the powers of darkness controlling this man was the most effective response.

We chose not to call the police, and we did not physically confront him. We just kept our hearts full of unconditional love and compassion toward him. Even in this extreme example, we clearly had a choice regarding whether or not to become offended at this person. We chose not to take up an offense or demand justice, because we recognized his condition and had no expectation that he would act justly towards us. We were able to successfully guard our "Achilles' Heel" and not become offended. Instead, our team members often sought out the man to give him food and offer to pray for him.

Offenses are all about the expectations that you hold toward someone. For this reason, the arrows of offense that do lodge in our hearts (or heals) have generally been aimed at us by people we never expected to fire arrows at all! The tragic truth is that most offense is given and taken between members of our own teams or churches, from and to our spouse or significant other, or between our leaders and us. The very people we are not prepared to defend against.

When you have an expectation that a person should not or would not offend you, then you are setting yourself up for failure. The truth is that we each have the potential to offend, probably on a regular basis. These offenses sometimes arise intentionally but more often come by complete accident or carelessness. You cannot control what arrows may come your way, but you can control whether or not you allow them to strike you and poison you. Like Achilles, you may be invincible in every other way, but a single poisoned arrow of offense could ruin you and destroy the potential of your team. You have to learn to overlook offenses.

How does offense destroy? In his excellent book on this topic, titled *The Bait of Satan,* author John Bevere says it this way.

"We build walls around ourselves when we become offended. Love does not go out and love does not come in, which results in selfishness, betrayal, and hatred. Offended people justify their behavior rather than repent of unforgiveness."

Offense cuts off the flow of love. If you cut off the offended person you are withholding your love. Love is the lifeblood of the family of God and without it your family will slowly perish. In the context of our discussion, the loss of this lifeblood, due to offense, will be the ultimate undoing of your team.

Here are some principles and practices that can help you live free from offense:

- Don't give the enemy a foothold into your life or your team. Ephesians 4:26-27 says, *"Be angry, and yet do not sin; do not let the sun go down on your anger, and do not give the devil an opportunity."*

    There will be multiple opportunities in the course of life with your team for you to take up an offense. Often there are hurtful things that have been done or said that could legitimately cause offense.

    If that arrow strikes for some reason, the challenge is to get it out of your 'heel' before it can poison you. The poisoning comes when you let it go unresolved, or as this scripture says, you actually give the devil an opportunity. What is the solution? Ephesians 4 indicates that you should resolve the issue the same day it happens. Don't let the day end with that poisonous arrow sticking out of your heel. Do what you need to do to talk with, forgive and release the offending person.

- *"Make every effort to live in peace with all men and to be holy; without holiness no one will see the Lord."* (Heb 12:14) Those who have hurt you may not ever accept responsibility for, or repent of, their hurtful words or actions. It doesn't matter. The resolution, forgiveness, and effort to deal with the offense is for your own wellbeing. You may not be able to bring about any kind of two-way reconciliation but you surely can make every effort to remove that arrow from your own heart before it kills you.

    The core of this principle is to live a lifestyle of keeping short accounts with other people and with God. If you find that you are taking on offense or giving offense regularly and you have never addressed the issue, you may also have many unresolved issues with God. The way you behave toward God's children is often a good indicator of the way you behave toward your heavenly Father.

- You have the ability to live free from offense regardless of what others do to you or say to you. As a person who has been 'recreated' or become a new creature in Christ Jesus, you are free to choose how you are going to respond to things in your life and environment that negatively affect you.

The key to complete freedom in life and in ministry is to realize that we don't have a 'right' to be offended. In a certain sense, Christians don't have 'rights' or 'entitlements'.

> *"You have heard that it was said, 'An eye for an eye, and a tooth for a tooth.' But I say to you, do not resist an evil person; but whoever slaps you on your right cheek, turn the other to him also. If anyone wants to sue you and take your shirt, let him have your coat also."* (Matt 5:38-40)

We are commanded by scripture to respond in the opposite spirit, to forgive and to 'turn the other cheek'. We don't have the right to punish those that hurt us or seek 'justice' against them. We have the privilege and 'right' to seek protection, vindication and healing from our heavenly father. We can trust that if we obey Christ and extend forgiveness and grace, we will enjoy a privileged place of freedom and joy that only a child of God can attain.

- Find out if you are the archer. It is likely that you have either intentionally or unintentionally been the archer who has loosed an arrow of offense at someone else. Develop a habit of checking your heart daily to see if you have any enmity against anyone, especially another believer, church member, ministry member, or team member. Often we are not our own best critics. By default we see ourselves in the best light possible and our souls are constantly trying to justify themselves and our behavior. The only way to truly know if you have hurt or offended someone is to humble yourself and ask them.

- *"A brother offended is harder to be won than a strong city, and contentions are like the bars of a citadel."* (Prov 18:19) You must be willing to invite people to speak into your life. When you don't you are the one who will suffer the most. The goal is to make things right daily. Don't let the sun go down on either your own anger or on anyone else's if it can be avoided. As this proverb says, it is extremely hard to win back a brother who has been offended. The shorter the amount of time that an arrow is lodged in a person's "Achilles Heel", the less opportunity the poison has to hurt them. Check your heart daily and go to your brothers and sisters daily and invite them to speak into your life and be open with you. Challenges to your Kingdom efforts come often enough. Do not make enemies of your closest allies.

- Keep things small.

> *"If your brother sins against you, go and show him his fault, just between the two of you. If he listens to you, you have won your brother over. But if he will not listen, take one or two others along, so that 'every matter may be established by the testimony of two or three witnesses.' If he refuses to listen to them, tell it to the church; and if he refuses to listen even to the church, treat him as you would a pagan or a tax collector."* (Matt 18:15-17)

This is one of the most important truths for dealing with relational issues within the body of Christ. The principle and practice taught here is that we must keep things to the smallest circle of affect when dealing with such issues. If there is a sin or an 'offense' against you, do not escalate the situation beyond you and the perceived perpetrator of the offense.

The first step to reconciliation commanded by this scripture, is that you go directly to the one who has sinned or offended you and try to make things right, just between the two of you. Do not post the issue on social media of any sort in order to gain public support for your position! That is in direct opposition to the teaching of Christ.

If you are not able to make progress between just you and the other person involved, only then are you to escalate the situation by one single step; by involving two or three witnesses to provide testimony. Not just one witness! Not just someone who is your best friend, who will always take your side, but multiple witnesses who can lend some objectivity to your perspective when the two of you share your perspectives.

It is not with the goal of these confrontations to prove that you are in the right and that you expect an apology. Rather, it is for the purpose of, *"making every effort, as much as it depends on you, to live at peace with all men."* (Romans 12:18) The goal of this confrontation is to get the poisonous arrow out of your heel and to take the opportunity to forgive and release the person you feel has harmed you.

The ultimate goal of the guidance in scripture is that relationship would be restored between members of the body of Christ who have wronged one another. Sometimes that ultimate aim is not attainable in the midst of the recovery from a harmful situation. In that case, your focus must be to, again, strive to live in freedom through the act of extending forgiveness and grace.

After you apply effort to obeying Jesus' teaching in Matthew 18, if the person you attempt to reconcile with totally rebuffs you, give him the same grace and freedom from expectation that you would give to a person on the street who has never met Christ. If the breaking of relationship results from the Matthew 18 process it is not a license for you to judge, ostracize, or condemn the other party. It is a license for you to take the full responsibility for the situation and provide the person with unlimited grace. The end of the process of escalation is that you get to love them unconditionally and through your love, help the person move towards a richer relationship with Jesus Christ.

The teachings of the Bible place the highest value in the Kingdom of God on relationships, relationship with God and relationships with others. Learning to live free from offense will make you strong in spirit, soul and body.

Make sure that you are living and thinking in such a way that your "Achilles Heel" is not vulnerable to the poisoned arrows of offense. Be certain that you are not an archer, and in as much as it depends on you, live at peace with all men. If you and your team can live by this Kingdom principle, you will see success and joy where most men fail.

Chapter 13
Survive or Thrive

HERE IS ONE LESSON I HAVE LEARNED during many outreaches around the world. I have discovered there are usually two primary dynamics that compel individuals to be involved in Kingdom work. One dynamic leads to just surviving, but the other mindset leads to thriving in your efforts.

> *"No longer do I call you slaves, for the slave does not know what his master is doing; but I have called you friends, for all things that I have heard from My Father I have made known to you."* (John 15:15)

I encounter many people who approach their ministry and relationship with Christ as if being a servant or a slave. If you find yourself viewing your work, ministry, and calling as only a task to be accomplished, you are working from a slave mentality. Servants, or slaves, as the Bible mentions, don't know why their master is doing what he does. They just do what they are told only out of obedience. This particular mindset leads to mere survival in life and ministry. It is a more transactional paradigm, in which we subconsciously say, "When I do what I'm told, I'll gain favor and reward from my master, boss, leader, pastor, parent, etc." If you embrace this mentality, your resulting actions reveal a weak understanding about who you are in Christ. The risk is in trying to gain favor, acceptance and reward from whoever we perceive to be our benefactor.

The person who thrives, on the other hand, has a different understanding of their identity and the nature of their Kingdom efforts. The biggest distinction is that the person who thrives is the one who knows what their Father is doing and does the will of their Father from a motivation of love, working as a son or daughter, not as a slave. The one who thrives is not working to complete a task for reward, but is working with their Father on what matters to their Father. Those who thrive have learned to work *from* a place of favor and reward, not *for* favor and reward.

"For we are His workmanship, created in Christ Jesus for good works, which God prepared beforehand so that we would walk in them." (Eph 4:10)

All of us who are in Christ Jesus are created for good works! Not works in the sense of trying to earn your way into Heaven, but works that God envisioned and prepared. Work that He would get to do with you.

One of the earliest records of God's interaction with Adam in the Garden of Eden illustrates this same concept. In Genesis 2:19 the Bible says, *"Out of the ground the Lord God formed every beast of the field and every bird of the sky, and brought them to the man to see what he would call them; and whatever the man called a living creature, that was its name."*

This scripture illustrates one of the wonderful ways God desires to love, honor, and interact with His people. Part of his original design for creation was for us to become co-creators with God himself. He intentionally left certain things unfinished to give us the opportunity to complete them. The beauty of this revelation is that we are able to understand and know God as a loving father instead of a taskmaster or slave owner. He is the one true Father who created us in His own image. He validates us and gives us the dignity of sons and daughters in His family. We must realize that our Heavenly Father's original design is that we will eventually be given the position of reigning with Christ Jesus. In fact, according to the apostle Paul, we are already, "seated with Christ in Heavenly places."(Eph 2:6)

This is part of the good news of the gospel! Not only do you have a physical passport and identity as a citizen of a particular physical country here on earth, but also you now have the ultimate second passport that takes you anywhere you want to go! Your second passport shows that you are a citizen of heaven.

By this understanding we know that each of our spirits actually live concurrently in two places at the same time! We are free from striving to get to heaven because once we have submitted our lives to Christ, we are given a seat in heaven and a new citizenship in the Kingdom of God. Understanding this new nature in Christ enables us to live from heaven toward earth instead of living from earth toward heaven.

The understanding that we gain through Ephesians 2:6 enables us to do the good works that we were created for without thinking those works are going to get us to heaven. Grace gives us access to relationship with God and the ability to be godly. The commonly understood definition of grace is, "unmerited favor." This is true, but it is also important to understand that grace is the operational power of God working in us to accomplish His Will in our lives. The purpose of the good works God prepared for us is that we would *bring* heaven to earth through those good works, not try to *get to* heaven through them.

Our co-laboring with Christ here on earth does not give us the idea that we are saved by works. It is actually by grace we are saved and by that grace we can do the work of causing his will to be done on earth as it is in heaven.

How is it possible that I could find myself in such a position of responsibility in the Kingdom of God? It is because the King adopted you and as such you were not only given a glorious inheritance, but you were also given responsibility in your Dad's Kingdom. The Bible says we are co-heirs with Christ in the Kingdom of God through the Spirit of Adoption that we have received.

> *"For all who are being led by the Spirit of God, these are sons of God. For you have not received a spirit of slavery leading to fear again, but you have received a spirit of adoption as sons by which we cry out, 'Abba! Father!' The Spirit Himself testifies with our spirit that we are children of God, and if children, heirs also, heirs of God and fellow heirs with Christ, if indeed we suffer with Him so that we may also be glorified with Him."* (Rom 8:14-17)

The good works that we were created for could be envisioned as the work we would do in a family business. Our Dad is the owner of the business, and his desire and design for the "God and Sons" company, AKA the Kingdom of God, is that he will one day place us in charge of what he has created.

In making us co-heirs with Christ Jesus, this is exactly what God has done. Your efforts (good works) in the Kingdom of God have to be approached from the understanding that you are already the son or daughter of a loving Father, and not the tool of a taskmaster. This understanding liberates us from a slave mentality and leads to believing we actually co-own the business as God's sons and daughters. Our Dad honors us and believes in us to such an extent that he puts us in charge of his belongings. You are royalty! You are responsible! You matter, and your outreach matters! Your efforts in your Dad's business are measures of the authority and responsibility that your Dad has delegated to you. He is confident in your identity as his son or daughter, he is confident in the Holy Spirit that is at work in you, and he is confident that his will can be accomplished through you!

To be one who thrives and not just a survivor you must know God deeply. Become so close to God that your heart begins to synchronize with His. It is here that you find yourself simply "knowing" what to do, how to do it, and why it needs to be done. From this place of intimacy with God, you know that you are already seated in heavenly places with Christ Jesus, you have received the Kingdom inheritance, and you are living from Heaven toward earth. How do you get close enough to God to live like this?

The first step is easy, James 4:8 says, *"Draw near to God and He will draw near to you. Cleanse your hands, you sinners; and purify your hearts, you double-minded."* You simply make the effort to draw near and God responds.

In his book "The Pursuit of God" A. W. Tozer, a great father in the Lord, said, "He (God) waits to be wanted." This is one of my favorite thoughts from Tozer. To really pursue God, to be one who thrives in relationship with God, begins with the effort of wanting God.

My first experience learning to live from heaven toward earth occurred while co-leading a team of young mission workers. We were doing an outreach to Brazil and Paraguay. It was my first field effort leadership role and I was only twenty years old. I had been serving as a staff member in a discipleship program for the first. It was a life-changing experience, and not least because I had the privilege of working alongside my father, as he led the discipleship program. It was a rare opportunity to glean from his long ministry experience and close relationship with the Lord. I grew tremendously during the experience.

As we departed for Brazil, I was sitting by myself on the long flight. I was experiencing a deep internal struggle and found myself intensely praying a very dangerous prayer. "God, I will do anything to draw close to you, I will do whatever it takes to know you." My heart was clinging to Psalm 25:14. *"The Lord is a friend to those who fear him. He teaches them his covenant."* (NLT)

I was desperate to know God and I felt strongly that He was prodding me toward pursuing Him to another level in my spiritual life. Never had I been satisfied knowing *about* God; but instead I wanted to *know Him* one-on-one. At any cost, I wanted to pursue God as described in James 4:8, and hold to the promise that is included in that scripture. In that section of Scripture James said, *"Draw near to God and He will draw near to you."*

"He made known His ways to Moses, His acts to the sons of Israel." (Psalm 103:7)

I wanted to know God's ways like Moses did. The sons of Israel had settled for just knowing about God's acts. Moses spoke face-to-face with God as a man speaks to his friend. The Old Testament tells how the sons of Israel were afraid and uncomfortable in the presence of God and chose to stand far off. They wanted Moses just to tell them to do whatever God instructed that they should do. I was not going to settle for standing far off to just let other people who *were* close to the Lord tell me what to do. I wanted to hear it straight from the Lord Himself.

God answered me clearly on that flight, to my great surprise. He said, "Oh really? You'll do whatever takes?" I responded, "Yes." I could almost hear him laughing out loud as he said, "Ok, I want you to get up at 4:00 AM every morning of this three-month trip, and seek me in the quiet place. If you do that, you will find me."

4:00 AM! At this point I was not an early riser, and God knew it would cost me to obey this request. "Ok," I said back to the Lord. "But here is my request, I'll get up at 4:00 in the morning and seek you if you will wake me up!" There was no alarm clock that would have been able to coax me out of bed for any reason at that point in my life. So, if I was going to do this, it had to be under the power of God. God said, "Ok, I'll wake you up."

On the first night of this outreach I found myself sleeping on a concrete floor in a half-completed building at a missions training center in Brazil. I was exhausted from the days of travel required to get there, and the schedule of the following day intentionally allowed for a late morning. We wanted to allow our team to sleep in and recover. Nevertheless, at 4:00 AM I was wide-awake. I sat up on my sleeping mat and realized that God had made good on His side of the deal. Rapidly, I got out of bed, grabbed my Bible and found a private place away from the rest of the sleeping team members. This began a season of unprecedented pursuit of God in my life.

As outreach progressed, I never missed a 4:00 AM morning, but it cost greatly. It cost me any evening social life with my team, or with friends we had made in Brazil. I had to force myself to go to sleep at 8:00 PM every night so that I would be functional the next day. Additionally, I often missed breakfast to have enough time to wait on the Lord in the mornings, but the reward was in every way worth the pain. I began to experience a new and different level of life and existence with God. Without even being conscious of the changes, I was beginning to view my life and earthly circumstances based on my true identity and position in heaven – living from heaven toward earth.

Other leaders on my team and even some of the team members began to take offense at me. They accused me of being hyper-spiritual. In retrospect, I think they must have been struggling with their own deep longing to draw near to the Lord and to find the kind of favor with Him that I had stumbled into. In truth, things in my life did get hyper-spiritual, and I believe this is the way we are all to live as Christians! I've heard it said that someone who is truly walking with the Lord should be, "naturally supernatural." I think this is a good description. As spiritual beings it is our heart's desire to be led by the Holy Spirit and to live from our identity as royalty seated in heavenly places with Christ Jesus.

God began to meet me each morning to teach me His ways and His preferences, and to share His thoughts with me. It really was incredible! There were some unexpected side effects to this intense season of pursuing God. Suddenly, I began to realize that I could anticipate what people were going to say and do, especially on my team. God gave me insight into the motivations and behaviors of the people and circumstances around me. Occasionally God would help me formulate a proper response to what someone was on his or her way to say to me in person. Alternatively, as soon as someone shared with me, I quickly received an inspired response or supernatural insight. This was one of the manifestations that began to offend my teammates, and led to their accusations that I was acting "hyper-spiritual." I was just beginning to tap in to the wisdom that is available for anyone who will truly press into the pursuit of Christ and live as though they are citizens of heaven.

God also began to give me divine wisdom that led to specific outreach strategies. At one point, our team was struggling with lack of direction and clarity about how to pursue our Gospel ministry in a particular city. This Brazilian city, contrary to our other experiences at that time, had very little openness to Christ. Our team was becoming discouraged. The Lord spoke to me, "Have the team gather and pray, asking for specific people to connect with today." On one occasion, as we were following the Lord's directions, he showed three of us an image of a young mother wearing a red sweater. Excited by the Lord's direction to us, our team divided into smaller groups and headed out into the city. We earnestly planned to find this young mother wearing a red sweater. After a couple of hours they had found this very person and offered to pray for her. She was in a desperate personal situation and needed a miracle. She also needed physical healing.

As our team members prayed for her, they were able to see her healed emotionally and physically. The young mother turned to Christ and her whole life was altered by this one encounter with heaven. From that time on, our team only wanted to seek God each morning to receive specific assignments from him. There was not a single boring or ineffective day of outreach after that!

Here are some comparisons that may help you recognize if you are thriving or just surviving:

Thriving	Surviving
1. Serves as a Son or Daughter	1. Serves as a Slave or Servant
2. Works from a place of favor and reward	2. Works for favor and reward
3. Knows what their father is doing and aligns with his will	3. Does only what they are told to do
4. Co-creates with God	4. Finishes the work as a task
5. Lives from Heaven toward Earth	5. Lives from Earth toward Heaven
6. Does 'good works' in Christ	6. Does the 'tasks' that are required
7. Looks to the Lord for guidance	7. Looks in the manual for the method to meet a known requirement
8. Knows God's ways	8. Knows about God
9. Worships and prays even if no one else will	9. Worships and prays when told to

As intense and rewarding as this season of pursuing God was, it ended as the outreach concluded. God made it clear to me that I had attained what I had prayed. I had moved to a completely different level of spiritual maturity and intimacy with God. My extreme, 4:00 AM quiet times were not to become a permanent feature of my life-style. But intensely prioritizing my relationship with God has become a life-style. I truly learned what it meant to thrive and not just survive. This type of experience with God is available to anyone who will pursue Him intensely.

Throughout your life as a follower of Christ, you encounter God given opportunities to respond to Him deeply and to move away from just surviving in life. You may recognize these opportunities by a deep sense of spiritual discontent and restlessness. These seasons are designed to make you uncomfortable so that you pray a dangerous prayer such as, "God, I will do anything to draw close to you. I will do whatever it takes to know you."

Chapter 14
The Circle of Trust

WHEN GOD CALLS YOU INTO A KINGDOM effort of almost any sort, it is likely you will find yourself on a team. There is very little that can be done effectively in the Kingdom on your own. You will find that God draws together a group of individuals to expand his kingdom through a particular assignment. This may be a short-term effort, such as a two-week missions effort, or you may find yourself on staff in a long-term ministry assignment. Maybe your assignment will be working for a company. You will have co-workers and clients and in those relationships you will discover this truth: *You must manage your circle of trust.*

A team is like a chain, each link of the chain is a team member, and the chain is only as strong as its weakest link. You might discover that you are the weakest link or you may find that others on your team are weaker yet. Despite the inherent weaknesses in your team or 'chain,' you are called to protect the group of people that God has entrusted to your care. You may not be the official leader of a particular team, but you are equally responsible for your contribution to team welfare, in God's eyes.

God uses this arrangement of being connected to one another and responsible for each other to establish you in a 'circle' or 'community' where you can thrive and where you can add value to others. He creates in you and in your team a "Circle of Trust" that is to be valued and managed.

I learned this concept the hard way during one of my outreaches to Ukraine. Our team was not a particularly mature group, but despite our many shortcomings, we had seen many miracles, divine interventions, and thousands of people respond to Christ during the first two months of this outreach.

One of the most memorable conversions we saw was that of a youthful Ukrainian couple named Vanya and Vika. Vanya was a heroin user and both of them made a comfortable living peddling illegal drugs in various

Ukrainian cities. They were actually a very sweet-natured and attractive young couple, and I would not have guessed their occupation from our first meeting.

Following a large city street evangelism event they both responded to the invitation and boldly received salvation. Their conversion was powerful and authentic. Vanya proceeded to throw his entire drug stash in a garbage can, right in front of us. He proclaimed he would never touch the stuff again. Vanya and Vika were radically saved, and as they spoke excellent English, they then began to help our group by translating for us. They helped us during many future ministry events. Unfortunately, we discovered the hard way that although someone may be saved, his or her process of sanctification could take awhile.

Members of our team began to be close friends with Vanya and Vika. Our team began to invite them to visit at our outreach housing facility. This led to considerable debate within our team. Certain team members, including me, were not comfortable with unknown people being welcomed into our circle of trust and security. The members of our team who had invited the couple to our housing area became angry. This led to a serious breakdown in team unity.

I had a sense that something was not quite right with the young couple. I could see they had professed Christ and made some obvious progress in their pursuit of God. But I sensed that they were not yet fully trustworthy. Soon my concerns became reality.

After their fourth visit, Vanya and Vika disappeared. Not only did they disappear, but so did most of the team's personal spending money. The young couple could not resist the temptation of unattended valuables in people's personal living areas, and so they cleaned us out. Fortunately, I had heeded the still small voice inside me that was warning me about the situation. I had kept my valuables hidden, and my room door locked at all times. There were only a few of us who avoided being robbed.

This development led to serious disunity and intense disagreement inside our team. Here is what happened. Our team, as a unit, did not sufficiently prioritize the security and interests of the mission that God entrusted to our care. Those members most at fault had violated the circle of trust by not considering the implications of their choices; how those choices would impact on their teammates, the other links in the chain. Our team relationships were a disaster. Our team fell apart. Our circle of trust was far from strong and instead resembled the strength of a wet noodle.

It is imperative that we each attend to the interests of the people for whom God has given us primary responsibility. Normally this would be your innermost circle, including your family, friends, and team members. As an extension and corollary of this primary responsibility, inner circle spaces are high trust areas. These high trust areas include places such as sleeping quarters, private team meetings or corporate team meals. These inner circle areas should not be violated. You need to seek unanimous agreement from all the stakeholders in your circle of trust before you bring an outside person into that context. This may seem like common sense, but I have seen it derail and disrupt more teams than almost any other single issue.

> *"After I looked these things over, I stood up and said to the nobles and the officials and the rest of the people, "Do not be afraid of them. Remember the Lord, who is great and awesome, and fight for your kin, your sons, your daughters, your wives, and your homes."* (Neh 4:14)

One way to think about your responsibility toward the people that God has called you to, is to look at the way Nehemiah challenged the Israelites while they were rebuilding the walls of Jerusalem. The enemies of Israel were all around, threatening, conspiring and attempting to disrupt the work that God had called Nehemiah and the Israelites to complete.

Like the ancient Israelites, you too have been called to certain, important work and you also have an enemy who is seeking to stop you at all costs. Nehemiah's challenge to his people was in order to protect their circle of trust and the work that their team was called to complete.

Nehemiah called the Israelites to remember the Lord, their brothers, sons, daughters, spouses and property. I believe that if we apply this principle to our own team context we will be able to overcome any enemy who comes against us. It will enable us to complete the good works that we are called to in Christ Jesus.

What are some keys to successfully managing your circle of trust and protecting your team?

- Live transparently. Living transparently is only possible if you are walking in humility.

- Be humble and accountable. It's hard to knock someone down if they are already bowed down.
- Admit that you are weak and that you need input from others. Proverbs 24:16 says, *"for though a righteous man falls seven times, he rises again."* We all struggle at times, and we all experience seasons of weakness. We are able to rise again according to scripture and because we are empowered by grace. The humility to admit you are weak and to lean for support on your brothers and sisters in Christ will drastically limit the number of times you have to 'rise again.'
- Stay integrated and engaged with your team or community. *"A man who isolates himself seeks his own desire; he rages against all wise judgment."* (Prov 18:1)
- Stay approachable. You are not your own best critic and you need input from other people, especially from those who love and value you. If you are insecure or hostile toward input, you will end up being isolated. That is not a good place to be. You must let others speak into your life even if their input is sometimes not especially helpful. If you can receive other people's input, it is a sign of a healthy soul, so keep the strong that is shared and move past what is weak.
- Create a culture of honor toward one another and mutual responsibility for your team. Don't ignore a weak link in your chain, your circle of trust. Pay attention to someone who is becoming weak and seek to encourage and strengthen that person. If your circle breaks, you break, and your work in the kingdom will suffer.

Chapter 15
Stay Covered

OUR TRAIN HAD ARRIVED, AND WE WERE exhausted. This remote North Indian town had become a common stop-over place for world travelers heading to Kashmir by railway. The train arrived four hours later than scheduled and we stepped out into the dead of winter. The environment was surreal. The cold low lying fog covered everything as the smoke from burning fires tried to mix with the clouds. There was just a little clear air and it let the temperature rapidly drop. Did I mention the cold?

As we journeyed towards Kashmir the world around us looked like a World War II old-fashioned color movie. Tanks and military vehicles lined streets, and soldiers camped in sprawling tent cities. They were gathering to move toward the conflict zone in Kashmir. The equipment and uniforms also appeared to be from World War II, and the whole scenario had begun to make us feel that we had somehow traveled back in time.

This particular city was located on the edge of the conflict zone. By 1998 it already had a reputation for being home to many radical Islamists who would jump at an opportunity to kidnap wayward foreigners, or worse. As the team leader I had taken every precaution possible to ensure the safety of my team and that we would arrive in Kashmir unmolested. However, the late arrival of our train had really complicated my plans. We had not intended to overnight in this area. Now that we had missed our connecting train to Kashmir, we had no choice about it.

As I surveyed the dismal, run-down condition of the train station, I concluded there was no way we could remain at this location overnight, waiting until our train left in the morning for Kashmir. The train station was cold, dirty, and crawling with questionable characters. These men would commit robbery given any opportunity. My teammate Mark and I quickly left the massive train station to find a hotel, or at least to attempt it. By God's grace, not far up the street we found a large house that doubled as a hotel for travelers. They had two large rooms they could rent to us and it was within reasonable walking distance from the train station.

We formed a plan to bring most of the team back to the hotel on foot, while leaving two team members to guard our pile of luggage. We would then arrange to transport our luggage and the remaining team members to the hotel via taxi. In India it is usually not possible to drag your bags through the streets that are covered by debris and mud. Our plan seemed reasonable, and the team agreed to it quickly. I chose the most mature team member, Jeff, to stay with the luggage, along with one of the girls from the team.

Jeff had a lot of life experience and was a few years older than I, but this was his first time serving in this sort of Kingdom effort. He was over-confident and self-willed to some extent, but I thought that with his age and maturity he would be the one to responsibly guard the luggage. I also left Jenny, a 19-year-old team member with Jeff in order to ensure that one person could continue to watch the bags in the event that one of them needed the restroom before we returned. My one instruction was, "Don't leave this area until I return, we will get the bags and take you guys in taxis to the hotel."

Part of the challenge of this particular situation was that we had disembarked on the third set of railroad tracks, in an outer part of the train station. This particular platform could only be reached by hiking up and down multiple sets of stairs to cross each preceding train platform. There was no way we were going to get our luggage and equipment back to the main entrance of the train station without hiring some local workers to haul it. Jeff and Jenny had no way of moving that huge pile of luggage by themselves, and my one instruction was to wait for me to return with the hired helpers.

After depositing our team at the tiny hotel, Mark and I returned with the hired luggage carriers only to find that Jeff, Jenny and the luggage were nowhere in sight. I urgently asked the police officers standing at the main station platform if they had seen any foreigners come over the stair bridges with a large amount of luggage. No one had seen anything. By this time, it was 1:00 AM and the station was nearly deserted, so they could not have been missed. Using these stair bridges was the only way out of the station.

Now, I was worried. Mark and I fanned out, down the far station platform where we had left Jeff and Jenny, looking for any evidence of where they may have gone. I found a police officer who spoke some English and he took up the cause with me to locate our missing team members. We found an old man sitting on the platform and asked him if he had seen anything. I felt a strong sinking feeling develop in my soul as he described seeing Jeff and Jenny walking off the end of the platform with some unknown men who were wheeling a cart full of our luggage. They had disappeared into the blackness of the night, headed in the opposite direction of the train station exit. My worst fears seemed to be coming true… some of my team members had potentially been kidnapped by extremists and taken off to who-knows-where. This was officially becoming the worst day of my young career as an outreach team leader.

Again Mark and I decided to split up, each of us being accompanied by an English-speaking police officer. Our plan was to search the remote areas behind the train station and then to circle around back, into the city buildings. After three hours of searching, we still had not found them, and had no idea what to do next. The officers and station officials had no further ideas, and I was minutes away from calling our ministry director in the USA to tell him that I had lost two students. This was not a call I wanted to make at all.

I suddenly felt I should pray one last time. I asked God to give me direction and wisdom to know where to find my students. Immediately, I had a clear word from the Lord in my mind that I should walk through the massive military encampment area to search among the rows of parked trucks. I had previously avoided this area because it seemed quite unlikely that our team members would not have been noticed. I began to jog as I searched through the muddy openings between trucks, while frantically looking around for any sign of my students.

I could not imagine what might have happened or why it appeared that they willingly went along with the men who led them into the darkness. Unexpectedly a woman wearing a full burka, the head and face covering worn by traditional Islamic women, appeared in front of me out of the darkness. She pulled down her veil and whispered, "Jon, it's me!" It was Jenny! I didn't know whether to be angry or melt with relief. I said, "Where is Jeff?" She started to cry and apologize. "We can talk about it later," I said. I was just relieved that she was ok.

Jenny led me through a maze of side streets, to an alley where I found Jeff nervously seated on a pile of luggage and feeling extremely sheepish.

Eventually, I learned their story. Jeff had become impatient with the plan to wait for our return, and had decided that he would do things his own way. He had hired a couple of local men to help haul the luggage off of the station platform.

Some local people had convinced him that there was a short cut around the end of the station platform that would allow them to cross over the tracks instead of hauling the luggage up and down multiple flights of stairs. Jeff went along with it, not knowing any better. This information matched the report we had received of Jeff and Jenny disappearing into the darkness with a group of local men. Unfortunately, the local help they had hired turned out to be swindlers.

With the money in hand the swindlers moved Jeff, Jenny and the luggage more than a mile away from the train station. Then the men left them stranded in some unknown alley with no way to get back to the train station or to reconnect with the rest of our team. Jeff couldn't go looking for us because he couldn't leave Jenny by herself, in full view of the many drunken taxi drivers. Further, Jenny would not be safe roaming the streets in the middle of the night by herself. If they both went searching all the team luggage would be stolen immediately. They had no options. Finally, they decided the only course of action was for Jenny to put on a burka and slip into the darkness heading toward the train station. By God's grace she found us.

Jeff learned a tough lesson that night about obedience and authority. Fortunately, he had full revelation that his rebellion and pride had led them into a very dangerous situation, and I never had to say a word about it. He totally revolutionized his attitude and became an amazing, servant-hearted team player during the rest of that outreach. Jeff went on to do significant long-term ministry in a difficult area of the world, and truly benefited from the lessons he learned on this particular field assignment.

In my experience, many serious problems and negative incidents that happen on outreaches are directly connected to the issue of authority.

One of the most important lessons you can learn is that authority and leadership are established by God for your benefit. The Bible says in Hebrews 13:17, "*Obey your leaders and submit to their authority. They keep watch over you as men who must give an account. Obey them so that their work will be a joy, not a burden, for that would be of no advantage to you.*"

You must come to understand the way God's government works in human affairs. Rebuffing this understanding can cause you to tolerate or initiate rebellion in your own life. This can lead to much unnecessary suffering. Let's take a look at how God's Kingdom operates, and how to relate to authority and leadership.

The fundamental understanding to be gained is that God governs and manages His creation though delegated authority. From the very beginning, God made this clear in the way that he placed Adam and Eve in the Garden of Eden.

Genesis 2:15 records this plan. *"Then the Lord God took the man and put him into the garden of Eden to cultivate it and keep it."*

From the beginning, God gave mankind authority, responsibility and stewardship over his creation and his purposes in human history. When Adam and Eve sinned, they yielded their authority to the devil by submitting to him instead of to God. For thousands of years Satan worked to challenge and thwart God's plans for creation. God's original authority structure was not re-established on the earth until Jesus died on the cross. The apostle Paul explained in Colossians 2:15. *"When He had disarmed the rulers and authorities, He made a public display of them, having triumphed over them through Him."*

A fascinating aspect of these historical events is this. After Jesus' victory at the cross, he turned around and gave his authority back to mankind. Matthew 16:19 reports his words. *"I will give you the keys of the kingdom of heaven; and whatever you bind on earth shall have been bound in heaven, and whatever you loose on earth shall have been loosed in heaven."*

The apostle Paul speaks to this issue of authority in Romans 13:1-2 when he says, *"Every person is to be in subjection to the governing authorities. For there is no authority except from God, and those which exist are established by God. Therefore, whoever resists authority has opposed the ordinance of God; and they who have opposed will receive condemnation upon themselves."*

The apostle Peter also makes this clear in 1 Peter 2:13-14 where he says, *"Submit yourselves for the Lord's sake to every human institution, whether to a king as the one in authority, or to governors as sent by him for the punishment of evildoers and the praise of those who do right."*

To really understand authority with a spiritual perspective, you can think of yourself as being under a multi-layered shield that shelters you from the attack of the enemy. This shield of protection is formed much like the ancient Greek *Phalanx*. Consider this explanation of these efforts.

> *"The phalanx formation was a close-rank, dense grouping of warriors armed with long spears and interlocking shields... The strength of the Greek phalanx lay in the endurance and discipline of the soldiers who made up the closely-packed rectangular formation of shields and spears. Once the phalanx was formed the soldiers would advance slowly toward the opposing army, fending off missile blows with their shields and holding the formation tightly in order to break through the ranks of the other side."* (Ancient History Encyclopedia—The Greek Phalanx—by Joshua J. Mark, 18 January 2012)

God forms a Phalanx of authority over you as protective armor for your body, soul and spirit. In my understanding, there are five distinct shields that form the phalanx God has ordained with the purpose of governing His creation and keeping you safe.

- **Parents:** By God's original design we all would be sheltered and protected by our parents as they raise us in the hostile environment found on earth.
- **Pastors:** You could also call these people *Spiritual Leaders*. God intends for all of us to be under the care of spiritual leaders who cover and protect us as we grow in the midst of a hostile spiritual environment.
- **Leaders:** Certain forms of leadership are in authority over us during the various seasons of life. We all experience this. We have Employers, Outreach Leaders, Teachers, Coaches and others who are in a position of responsibility during particular assignments. Leaders are often responsible for covering and protecting us in different aspects of life, in both the spiritual and natural realms of life. Leaders are God's Kingdom governors who, through courage and service, are responsible for implementing the plans of God for the earth.
- **Civil Government:** God makes it clear in 1 Peter 2 that He has established earthly government systems to reward righteousness and punish evil. They are charged as ministers to administrate the people and systems of the world.

Authority and leadership are designed to be a conduit from God that allows blessing to flow down from Him, through your leaders, to you, and then on down to those you lead. Choosing to stay covered by God's phalanx, and submitting to leadership are shields that God has created for us. We don't have to bear the constant onslaught of the enemy alone. If you are missing one of the shields in the Phalanx, you are vulnerable to the attacks of the enemy in that area.

Remember the explanation of spiritual warfare in Ephesians 6:16 which says, *"above all, taking the shield of faith with which you will be able to quench all the fiery darts of the wicked one."*

We were born into in a spiritual conflict zone. The enemy daily directs fiery darts toward us. We must choose to remain covered. Rebellion, or attempts to avoid authority and accountability in life, will diminish these vital shields; the very things that God intends for our protection.

When we finally arrived in Kashmir it really was the dead of winter. The combination of hazy, grey skies, leafless trees and dust gave the normally beautiful region an apocalyptic feel. The World War II-era feel of the environment became even more pronounced as roads and intersections were lined with Indian military emplacements protected by sandbag walls. This area of the world was in a volatile phase. India controls the region, yet, Pakistan, China and Afghanistan all border Kashmir. Armed struggle for territorial control, and the vastly different political and religious ideologies have made circumstances miserable for the Kashmiri population. We discovered that militant and insurgent activity were a regular occurrence, even though India tried to keep peace using a sizable military presence.

For safety, our team decided to live on one of the many beautifully hand-carved houseboats anchored in the lake on the edge of Srinagar. It was bitterly cold, and the lake already had two inches of ice. To reach our houseboat, and to return to shore each day, we embarked on small rowboats. The boatmen propelled the boats forward by forcing them through the ice flows. First they break the ice in front of the boat, and then they paddled forward a few feet at a time. Each night was a bizarre, moonlit boat ride back through the ice to our palatial wooden houseboat. However, as romantic and idyllic as that sounds, our houseboat was heated with only a small, central wood stove, and the structure was completely uninsulated. Essentially, it was as cold inside as it was outside. We lived in these conditions for nearly two months.

During this time, some of the younger students began to allow a rebellious attitude to develop. Two 20 year old women, in particular, began to habitually disobey during certain team-related activities. To further complicate the situation, they tried to hide it, and they lied to me. I was becoming concerned for them, because I understood the principle of staying covered. I knew that removing oneself from the protection of the authority that God has provided is dangerous even under normal circumstances; and we were in far more dangerous circumstances at the time.

One night, the team returned to our houseboat after an entire day out in the villages surrounding the main city. I established two smaller teams for ease of ministry, and to help us keep a lower profile. Local religious militants had been very active that week.

The smaller team I led that day returned first, and we waited for the second group to arrive. Then we could begin our daily, pre-dinner debrief. The second group finally arrived, but the two young women I mentioned were not with the group. When I asked about them, my assistant leader informed me that they had insisted on remaining behind at the market to "do some shopping." I was seriously concerned. This area was dangerous, and two American girls out on their own at the market was a situation begging for trouble.

Hours later, these two girls arrived at our houseboat home in tears. I could see that they were incredibly upset and tears were flowing. "What happened?" I asked. They began to confess.

One of the rules of our discipleship program was that students could not acquire any new body piercings during the program. We did not want to send students back to their home churches with a collection of piercings acquired during our program. These girls had begged me for a week to let them go and get their noses pierced at the local market. I had repeatedly told them that this was not going to be allowed.

After pretending to relent, they tricked their team leader into allowing them to remain behind in the market so they could get their noses pierced that evening. They reasoned that once it was done, there was nothing that anyone could do about it. In this action they had chosen to remove themselves from the shielding protection that God had placed them in.

On the way back to the dock to catch their boat ride home, their lack of protection became obvious to them. They were riding along in a small, three-wheeled vehicle called a 'rickshaw.' These common taxis are essentially a three-wheeled motorcycle or large tricycle, with a small passenger space built over the back.

As the girl's rickshaw raced past the front of a central military establishment, explosives were thrown from another rickshaw carrying Islamic militants traveling in the opposite direction. The explosives aimed at the nearby military bunker detonated just 20 feet behind our team members. The force of the explosion lifted their rickshaw into the air. It flipped over onto its side, and slid to a stop.

By God's grace our two team members were not seriously injured, but the explosion had stunned them and caused temporary hearing loss. By the time they made it back to the houseboat they were fully aware of the risks they had taken through stepping out from the protection that God had provided.

Listening to their story, and their very deep repentance, I felt the kindness of God toward these young women. They had learned an important life lesson - the hard way. Our entire team forgave them and prayed for them and I never had to say another word about the incident. Following their narrow escape, they showed positive change and were very effective, serving diligently during the rest of our outreach.

Leaders and other authority figures are in positions of responsibility over God's creation and purposes. God intends that as part of their responsibilities they will oversee and serve you. Leaders are in your life to protect you and to help guide you along toward your calling and potential in God. Their main role is often to buffer you against events in life that would normally be devastating. Learn to stay covered and stay protected!

Even if you are having a hard time with a particular leader or authority figure in your life, don't let it lead to rebellion. It is probable you will encounter situations in which you need to work with a difficult or flawed leader. Parents are not perfect, governments are often corrupt, and leaders are sometimes insecure and may have other weaknesses. However, God is in the process of restoring our fallen world, so even if you feel that things are so difficult that you can't trust the authority you are under, trust God who is at work in them and through them, and pray often for your leaders. (1 Timothy 2:1-3)

If you find yourself in a context where your leadership is sinning or is so dysfunctional that it is causing damage to you or others, you should do something about it. If the leader in question is a Christian, then definitely follow the biblical teaching of confrontation and reconciliation. First go directly to them!

"If your brother sins, go and show him his fault in private; if he listens to you, you have won your brother. But if he does not listen to you, take one or two more with you, so that by the mouth of two or three witnesses every fact may be confirmed. If he refuses to listen to them, tell it to the church; and if he refuses to listen even to the church, let him be to you as a Gentile and a tax collector." (Matt 18:15-17)

As we earlier discussed in this book, remember that if the person is not receptive, or refuses to listen, the scripture clearly instructs you to change the way you relate to the person. In this scripture it says to treat them as a tax collector or Gentile. This is about people who are sinners are separated from God needing salvation. The Matthew 18 pattern does not mean that you should ostracize or shun the person. Rather, you no longer have the expectation that they will behave like Christ. Attempt to reach your brothers and sisters in Christ with the unconditional love of Christ, and see them come to repentance, moved by the grace of God. It is a grace response, not a judgment response that is called for by this passage.

If your leadership is not submitted to the authority of scripture then you can't have the same expectations and standards that you would have for someone who is walking with God. In an outreach or ministry context we hold ourselves, and the brothers and sisters we work with, up to the standard of Christ. If a Christian leader is unapproachable and unrepentant then you have to take responsibility for your own wellbeing and make some changes in your life. One of life's most important principles is that you are not able to change others but you do have the responsibility to change yourself.

Don't try to change your leader, but ask God what changes you need to make to either help the situation or to move into a different healthy environment. God is able to fix things in people's lives even when they may seem unfixable. Ultimately, it is God who is able to help and restore leaders who are making a mess of things. Romans 14:4 says, *"Who are you to judge the servant of another? To his own master he stands or falls; and he will stand, for the Lord is able to make him stand."*

Leaders are God's servants, and God establishes all authority. Trust God in your leaders even if they aren't trustworthy. It is important to recognize that God operates through delegated authority. If God has called you to a particular organization, team, or effort, you will also find yourself called to obey the leadership and authority that God has appointed.

To be successful, you must choose to honor people for who they are and not judge them for who they are not. God is raising you up to be a leader. In fact, you are already a leader. What you have authority over right now may seem insignificant, but it is not. Remember Jesus' parable of the talents. *"His master replied, 'Well done, good and faithful servant! You have been faithful with a few things; I will put you in charge of many things. Come and share your master's happiness!'"* (Matt 25:21)

In this parable the faithful servants who were pleasing to the master acted as good stewards over all they had been entrusted with. They each began with being responsible for a few pieces of money, and the faithful servants were rewarded with even more responsibility.

You will be given authority over certain aspects of God's kingdom plans and purposes as you show yourself faithful with what He has already delegated to you. However, you must learn to follow well before you can lead well. You must learn to trust God in others as God begins to trust you.

Chapter 16
The Lay of the Land

"For our struggle is not against flesh and blood, but against the rulers, against the powers, against the world forces of this darkness, against the spiritual forces of wickedness in the heavenly places." (Eph 6:12)

I WAS ON MY WAY TO ISRAEL and Albania for a three-month outreach. Happily, I had the chance visit my friend Mike in Oxford, England. It was a great opportunity to visit one of my close friends. We had traveled the former Soviet Union together and faced some real challenges as we were on outreach. Mike was now studying at the University of Oxford and had invited me to stay for a few days. A pleasant recuperation before I headed on to the next phase of my trip. After a year we were excited to reconnect but little did I know this relaxing stop-over was about to take on a very spiritual dimension. It was on a level the likes of which I had never before encountered.

Mike's ground floor studio apartment was tiny. He lived just off the central quad at his particular college in Oxford. Here, I was immersed in the traditions and the historic almost other-worldly culture of this institution. In addition to the time we spent catching up, Mike and I attended the common meals. We joined the other students, one of whom would be randomly selected to pray over their meals. They prayed in Latin. It was quite an experience.

I was introduced to a number of Mike's friends and fellow students during my short stay. As I got to know these students my heart began to break with grief over the lost condition of their souls. A drug-filled hopelessness seemed to pervade their lives. One Friday night, near the end of my visit, students began to fill the quad after dinner. This was the usual location for them to begin partying and relaxing before the weekend. Dozens of students were drinking heavily, and drugs were used openly.

When Mike and I returned to his apartment after dinner, we passed through the revelry-filled quad. Mike expressed the same grief I was already feeling. We mourned his fellow student's destructive choices. "I've got to do something," Mike said. "I'm going to stay out here and try to talk to people." I was glad he was up for the challenge. He seemed to be the only level-headed person in the area at that time. Because I had to catch the 5:00 AM bus back to London, I let Mike know I was going to head back to the room to get some rest.

In the one-room apartment was a single bed, a small table, two chairs and a lounge chair stationed at the end of the small bed. Mike had graciously given me the bed, while he slept in the middle of the floor using just a pile of blankets for a mattress.

I didn't know how to deal with the grief and heart felt compassion I had for the aimless students who were gathered outside. I decided the appropriate thing was to worship. I tuned up the guitar I traveled with and began to quietly play a simple song of prayer. This particular song was a simple but powerful song of declaration and intercession. The lyrics go like this:

"God of the needy, God of the poor … The God of justice, the God of right … Help me not be late… help me not be late."

I quietly sang this song as a prayer over the students. It was an intercessory appeal that God would help Mike and me to be faithful strong witnesses. Then I found myself pulled into a deep, spiritual connection with God. I lost the awareness of time and felt that my physical body had been completely shut out of what was happening. I think my spirit was worshipping in heavenly places.

Abruptly, I 'came to', glanced at my watch, and realized I had been worshiping and praying for five hours! It was nearly midnight! Although it seemed I had just begun to sing, I had lost track of the hours while I was deep in the presence of God. I put my guitar away and went straight to bed. Now I was only going to have five hours of sleep before leaving to catch my bus. Shortly after I lay down on the bed, Mike quietly came in and crawled into his bed on the floor. I was so tired, I didn't say anything to him, and just closed my eyes.

As I closed my eyes, I found myself standing in Mike's Oxford apartment but the room was lit with a glowing light that seemed to come from all directions at once. I was standing by the small table in the room and looking toward the door and window that faced the quad. Suddenly, the door burst open and a man forcefully advanced toward me. The man was dressed in a white, cricket player's uniform, and was exceedingly handsome and had golden, tanned looking skin.

As he walked toward me, my eye was drawn to the name embroidered on his shirt. The embroidered name read "Oxford". I examined his face as he moved right up to me. He pointed his finger in my face and said with deep fury, "You really hurt me." "Good!" I said. He repeated it again with a seething anger, "You really hurt me." Smiling now, I repeated my response, "Good!" I exclaimed.

"Who do you think you are? These students belong to me!" he said. He circled around me with his finger still in my face. As I faced him he adamantly asserted his claims and rights over the students. "Who do you think got these students into prep school? Who do you think helped them get the grades? They are mine and they are here for my purposes!" he asserted.

I had no fear. I was smiling at him and a power I had never experienced rose up within me. I was completely *in the spirit*. I think it was like what the Apostle John reported in Revelation 1:10, "I was in the Spirit on the Lord's day..."This was the spiritual realm and my spirit was confronting a spiritual ruler. In this completely spiritual state I realized I was confronting the 'principality' of Oxford and he was angry.

Principalities are spiritual powers that seek to control people, places and institutions. As his assertions and claims continued I was able to strike down each of his arguments with specifically quoted portions of scripture. The Holy Spirit prompted these scripture references. The scriptures seemed new to me. I had no conscious memory understanding them in a way that would defeat this enemy. Each of his claims was deflected or countered as scripture flowed out of me. One particular quote finally silenced his assertions. *"For I know the plans that I have for you," declares the Lord, "plans for welfare and not for calamity to give you a future and a hope."* (Jer 29:11)

Now he was furious. We circled each other in the room filled with spiritual light. Finished with verbal arguments, he suddenly reached out and locked me in a sort of wrestling move. Each of us had an arm reaching around the other's head. We continued in this mutual headlock circling each other, much like the start of an Olympic style wrestling match. In this spiritual conflict he could not overpower or harm me. Although I could not overpower him I laughed aloud at his attempts throw me to the floor.

I remembered this kind of grappling from my high school wrestling matches. There seemed to be nothing my opponent could do to master me. He was raging with fury now. Finally, he broke off the engagement and stormed back out the door. The door slammed behind him and I suddenly sat straight up in bed, my heart racing. The clock was flashed 5:00 AM as Mike said in a loud whisper, "Jon! Are you awake?"

I *was* awake, and my mind was racing, trying to catch up with my spiritual awareness. "Jon!" Mike said again. "You're never going to believe this!" "Try me," I whispered.

"I came in and lay down," Mike said. "As I turned off the light, the door opened, a man came in and in the dark sat at the end of your bed. He just now stood up and left! What is going on?" Mike demanded to know.

I reported on my own visionary experience. He had seen in the physical realm, a small part of the encounters I had in the spiritual realm. Mike had been able to physically see the 'principality' of Oxford while I was engaged with this being in the spiritual realm. We were both staggered as I quickly packed up and headed for the bus station. Mike and I parted ways at the bus stop after an unexpected encounter that night.

Some ten years later, I befriended a young man who had been an Oxford student at the time of this encounter. I didn't know him at the time of my visit, but as we compared notes about this story years later, he came to some clear conclusions.

He told me that prior to the time in question, the Christian Unions and other student ministries in the area had been struggling to even survive. Their student participation had dropped to historic lows. As we narrowed down the time frame of the encounter with the 'principality' of Oxford, we discovered that there had been a sudden spiritual revolution in many students at about the same time. Attendance at the Christian Student Union jumped from 40 to 400. None of the Christian student leaders could account for the sudden change. He rejoiced to learn that a powerful experience of prayer seemed to release the spiritual revival experienced by the Oxford Christian Community at that time.

The term, "The Lay of the Land," is a common American idiom. In its usual context, it means to take in or understand the general state or condition of affairs under consideration, or the facts of a situation.

We have to understand the Lay of the Land when going into any Kingdom enterprise. We should recognize that no matter what the nature of our outreach is, we will primarily be plundering the house of the strongman. Jesus' comments on this process are recorded in Matthew 12:29. *"Or how can anyone enter the strongman's house and carry off his property, unless he first binds the strong man? And then he will plunder his house."*

What does it look like to part the strongman from his possessions?

When we engage the spiritual strongman of any region, expect to encounter a belligerent enemy who asserts his claim to possessions that, in truth, actually belong to the King of Kings. The strongman is not about to be parted from his property, unless the representatives of the King who is reclaiming His Kingdom exert a certain measure of God's authority and power against him.

We are a commissioned officer of Heaven and a son or daughter of the King of Kings.

"And Jesus came up and spoke to them, saying, "All authority has been given to Me in heaven and on earth. Go therefore and make disciples of all the nations, baptizing them in the name of the Father and the Son and the Holy Spirit, teaching them to observe all that I commanded you; and lo, I am with you always, even to the end of the age." (Matt 28:18-20)

We are granted authority and power by the authority or *government* that is above us. The King in whose Kingdom we have citizenship commissions us. What is the purpose of our commission in the Kingdom?

Without a commission from the authority above him, an officer of the law might be able to put on a weapon and uniform but he would have no authority to enforce the law, and if he tried to do so without authority, he would actually be breaking the law. A commission bestows legitimacy. The commission we have received from Jesus is for the purpose of parting the strongman from the property he has laid claim to, God's property. Understanding who we are and that we are commissioned, will give us confidence and boldness to carry out the will of the Lord in His Kingdom.

Since we have been co-missioned with Christ we are on the same mission as Christ. We are co-laboring, co-working, co-operating, co-designing and co-missioning with Christ. But, what is He working on? What was Christ's mission? *"The Son of God appeared for this purpose, to destroy the works of the devil."* (1 John 3:8b)

Jesus has all authority over every natural and spiritual object, force or entity, and now his disciples are empowered with His authority, to act as His agents, to carry out this great commission. Thus we understand, *authority*, but what is the purpose of *power*?

Remember, *"For the kingdom of God does not consist in words but in power."* (1 Cor 4:7)

We must combine authority, or 'commission' from God with the power of the Holy Spirit to enact true, spiritual enforcement in the Kingdom of God. All Christians have been commissioned with authority, but not all Christians realize that they also have the means of enforcement, the power of the Holy Spirit.

> *"For this purpose also I labor, striving according to His power, which mightily works within me."* (Col 1:29)

One of the great mysteries of the Kingdom of Heaven is that God is excited to prove His power and accomplish His purposes through those he has commissioned. This means all of us. By the power and action of the Holy Spirit and the work of Jesus Christ on the cross, once you are a new creation in Christ Jesus (2 Corinthians 5:17), you become a simple jar of clay to contain "this all-surpassing power" that is from God (2 Corinthians 4:7).

We were designed to be filled up and poured out, and to overcome. Isaiah 54:17 says, *"'No weapon that is formed against you will prosper; And every tongue that accuses you in judgment you will condemn. This is the heritage of the servants of the Lord, And their vindication is from Me,' declares the Lord."*

Victory is possible!

We are also promised victory. Just as Christ was victorious at the Cross we are promised that no weapon formed against us will prosper. If you learn to appropriate the all-surpassing power that God has made available to you and stand on the truths of scripture, we will discover that we were designed to overcome.

> *"And behold, I am sending forth the promise of My Father upon you; but you are to stay in the city until you are clothed with power from on high."* (Luke 24:49)

If we can simply begin to understand a disciples position in the Kingdom of God, we can approach our life and calling in such a different way. Instead of fatalistically cowering and saying, "if God wills," when the enemy tries to assert himself over and against God, we will remember who we are, and the authority and power we have received. The believer who knows who they are in Christ Jesus will stand up and destroy the works of the devil.

Failure is always an option!

Colossians 2:15 says, *"And having disarmed the powers and authorities, he made a public spectacle of them, triumphing over them by the cross."* (NIV)

Even though the enemy has ultimately been defeated, his kingdom is propped up by the willful, heedless and sometimes unwitting alignment of sinful actions with his will, by people who knowingly or unknowingly make him their king. Sadly, even Christians are able to re-empower a disempowered devil by submitting to him. Remember, the enemy has no authority over us… unless we give it to him. We can sign over our authority by aligning our will to his just as Adam and Eve did when they sinned in the Garden of Eden. Don't re-arm the disarmed enemy.

How could I find myself re-arming the enemy? "How in the world would I give authority back to the devil?" Romans 6:12-16 clearly explains how this can happen in the life of a believer. The passage says,

> *"Therefore do not let sin reign in your mortal body so that you obey its lusts, and do not go on presenting the members of your body to sin as instruments of unrighteousness; but present yourselves to God as those alive from the dead, and your members as instruments of righteousness to God. For sin shall not be master over you, for you are not under law but under grace. What then? Shall we sin because we are not under law but under grace? May it never be!* **Do you not know that when you present yourselves to someone as slaves for obedience, you**

are slaves of the one whom you obey, *either of sin resulting in death, or of obedience resulting in righteousness?"*

Our enemy is not threatened by someone who has become his slave. By the very nature of the illustration in Romans 6 it is clear that we choose who we are submitted to based on whether or not we "let sin reign in your mortal body."

During one outreach in Brazil, I had the privilege of working alongside some dynamic and powerful Brazilian evangelists. They were seeing tremendous fruit in their ministry as they roamed the streets sharing the gospel, healing people, and setting people free from demonic oppression. These men of God told me that one of their favorite activities was to ride the bus in order to look for demonized people. When they found a person who was possessed by demons, they first prayed for them to be delivered, then shared the gospel with them. Many, many people were rescued from he gates of hell by these ministers of the Gospel.

The reason they preferred to engage people while on the bus was because there was nowhere for the demonized people to run! The demons could not cause the person to flee from the evangelists, as they were all trapped together on the bus. This led to some wild commutes that I'm sure many Brazilians talked about later at work.

When I asked them how their street ministry had become so powerful and effective, they told me a story of learning about the correlation of authority and spiritual effectiveness. One day, when the three of them were walking down a crowded street, they came face to face with a demoniac. They proceeded to confront the spirit and command him to leave the oppressed person. Immediately, the demon responded, "you don't have authority over me!" Pointing at one of the three men it said, "I saw what you did just a few minutes ago down the street."

The demon refused to leave the man on legal grounds. The two other men said they looked at the man who was pointed out by the evil spirit and asked him, "What have you done?" The man immediately confessed that he had engaged in some form of sinful activity before joining the group. He proceeded to confess his sin and repent before God and his friends. Immediately, he then turned to the demonized man and again commanded the evil spirit to leave, and it left that instant. These three men had gone on to walk in true authority and were unhindered in their spiritual effectiveness from that day forward.

The principle is that you don't have authority over something you are submitted to. Romans 6:16 says, *"Do you not know that when you present yourselves to someone as slaves for obedience, you are slaves of the one whom you obey..."*

The question we have to ask is, "Whom do we obey?" Don't blame God for your lack of effectiveness on outreach. Don't take the path of least resistance and wave the white flag by saying fatalistic things like, "I guess it's not Gods will," when some work of the enemy refuses to bow the knee to Jesus. The Bible has already clearly stated in 1 John 3:8b, *"... The Son of God appeared for this purpose, to destroy the works of the devil."*

We already know what God's will is, but as He has chosen to work through His children, we really do matter in the effectiveness equation.

Don't be discouraged!

Don't be discouraged or overly concerned about the resistance we face from the enemy. Even as we recognize that we are facing opposition we should respond like the apostle Paul when he says in 1 Corinthians 16:8-9, *"But I will stay on at Ephesus until Pentecost, because a great door for effective work has opened to me, and there are many who oppose me."*

Paul was not discouraged or fearful of opposition. In fact, it seems to motivate him to take advantage of a great door for effective work. He also seems to be motivated to stay on in Ephesus *because* there are many who oppose him. We should have the same attitude when facing difficulty and opposition in both the natural and the spiritual realms.

Knowing is half the battle.

One of my favorite childhood cartoon shows on TV was the original G.I. Joe series. At each commercial break, there was often a word of advice or knowledge shared with the childhood audience. One such instruction was, "don't give your address to strangers," and other such useful admonitions for young people. The tag line following these instructions has remained with me. It said, "now you know... and knowing is half the battle." This tag line is just as appropriate for the topic of authority that we have just covered. Once you *know*, you are at least half-way to using that knowledge to succeed.

Now you *know* that Christ has given you His authority let's look at some of the enemy's tactics and how we should respond to them.

Know

- The devil knows you are coming
- He will test you to see if you are a threat
- He won't let you just walk in and take things from him without resistance
- He will attempt to test your defenses before you even get there
- He will try to tempt you here with the things that will subject you there
- If he can subject you here then you will be no threat to him there
- If you can walk in victory here you will overcome there

Be aware

- Pay attention and learn to identify the tests and attacks that come your way.
- Watch out if you begin to think and act abnormally.
- Have you, or your friends and family, noticed personality changes in you?
- Are you struggling with strange or abnormal thoughts and temptations?
- Have you begun to be easily offended?
- The enemy is trying to deceive you into aligning with him and handing over your authority.

Respond

- Lean into your relationship with the Holy Spirit for discernment, wisdom and guidance.

- We need each other, you can't make it on your own without community.
- We can't see the changes or warning signs in ourselves.
- We are not our own best critics and we need input.
- Don't judge or condemn each other as it is likely that the target of your judgment is being harassed spiritually, so don't react in the flesh but see with your spiritual eyes.
- Be gentle and loving with people, recognize that just like yourself, others on your team may be struggling as you prepare for your outreach.
- Identify the areas in which the enemy is attempting to bring you under subjection.
- Repent, resist and maintain your authority.
- Don't hand over your authority by aligning with the enemy of your soul through wrong thoughts or actions.

Chapter 17

When in the Wilderness

LIFE AND OUTREACH WILL ALWAYS HAVE THEIR wilderness seasons. Much of the course of your life will be affected by the choices you make when in the wilderness.

Our small tour bus slowly crept up the narrow, one-lane road that snaked its way through the Transylvania region of the Romanian Alps. At that time Romania was a broken and starving county six months after the overthrow of a Communist Dictator. Now the government was in disarray, barely functioning and food was in short supply.

There were 40 teenagers on this outreach team. Four days earlier we set out to cross Romania. Our route across the country was strongly influenced by our need to find food. We drove from city to town on a lengthy and very indirect path toward the border. It was slow and it was painfully hot. No air-conditioning was available and the temperature approached 100 degrees.

Worse, we couldn't travel at night because local bandits setup fake accidents to make motorists stop. Maybe it was an overturned ox cart or a crashed car. When an unsuspecting motorist stopped to help or was stuck in traffic behind the fake accident the bandits would rob the travelers. So, no cool nighttime driving could be done.

The journey had become extremely difficult for our team. The heat was stifling and we had not found sufficient food for several days. In one town our team narrowly escaped a riot. The riot started because we had purchased the last remaining food at a local restaurant. Drinkable water had not been part of our diet for days, so we had resorted to drinking canned juice and soft drinks that could occasionally be found.

In the bus two distinct factions began to form. The larger group of students had completely given themselves over to a bad attitude. They had raised the art of complaining to unprecedented heights. Even some of the adult team leaders had joined in the complaining and negativity without any attempt to constrain their behavior.

Then, in the back corner of the bus, there were six of us who created a no-complaining zone. We prayerfully committed to each other that we would not give into a bad attitude. We decided not to complain, no matter how difficult this trip became. My younger sister and I led the way in establishing the no-complaining zone. Even though this made us very unpopular, our small group, in the back of the bus, continually chose to move in the opposite spirit. Instead of joining the complaining we tried to be thankful and generous at every opportunity. As teenagers this was really challenging! Honestly, there was plenty for us to be *un*thankful for and to complain about. Much of the team had even started to murmur and grumble against our team leader, accusing him of all kinds of failings. The non-complainers-club in the back of the bus would not tolerate any accusations or grumbling against the leadership. This isolated us even further from the larger group.

As our bus crawled along through the Alps we began to grow hopeful because once we had cleared the high country, the Moldovan border was only a one-day drive away. Moldova, Ukraine and Russia at least held the hope of food for purchase. Then, on the downhill side of the mountain, we saw a tunnel ahead of us, and my heart began to sink with disappointment. There was no way our bus was going to fit through that tiny tunnel. Our vehicle was at least three feet too tall. As we pulled up and stopped in front of the tunnel, waves of disbelief and anger swept through the students on the bus. Even the non-complainers-club was tested nearly beyond limit by this development.

We held the line though, and determined to not give in to the prevailing attitude. The implications of our situation were clear. We were stuck in Romania. There was no way to proceed and no way to even turn the bus around. Slowly, the bus literally crawled backward up the mountain road in reverse. By the end of the day we reached the top of the mountain pass and found a pull out large enough in which to turn the bus around.

It was late in the day and darkness prevented us from driving back down the mountain. We decided to overnight in an abandoned camping facility we found just off the road. We planned to drive back the way we had come on the following day. We all hoped the new day would bring us to a new route to Moldova.

Then it got cold. When we prepared for this trip we had planned for temperatures that would exceed ninety degrees during the entire trip. No one had anticipated camping next to a glacier on the top of a mountain. Some team members only had Bermuda shorts and no one had brought a real coat of any kind. As the sun began to set, I knew we were in trouble. I had lived in Montana and love the summer high mountain camping trips. I knew that the temperatures at this altitude would drop radically at sunset. I tried to warn the team, but most rebuffed my urging to prepare for the cold.

Tents were set up and the team spread out to try to find water. Amazingly, nearby we found a flow of fresh water coming straight out of the side a glacier and filled a small lake. After four days in a hot bus with no showers, many students soon jumped into the water. It was an understandable decision, but I urged the team not to become chilled before the sun went down. Oh well, I tried.

Clean but shivering, the students crawled into their tents and prepared to sleep. I feared the team was severely unprepared and urged them to retreat to bus for the night. Inside the bus we could attempt to stay warm even though we couldn't run the engine since we were short on fuel. Shortly after about twelve of us piled into the back of the bus, the driver locked the door. Only then we found out the door could not be unlocked from the inside. Astoundingly the only way in or out of the bus was through the sliding window next to the driver's seat.

The sun set, and the cold set in. The temperature dropped more than sixty degrees; from above eighty degrees all the way to below freezing. We began to shiver violently. Desperately we emptied all the luggage we could find and made an enormous pile of clothes and towels and costumes in the back of the bus. Then we crawled under the pile and tried to stay warm. We were too cold to sleep, but we managed to avoid hypothermia.

The view out the window of the bus was like a scene from a horror movie. The rest of our team was visible in the foggy moonlight. Wrapped in their collapsed tents they wearily wandered the road next to the bus. Most of them were wearing only flip-flop sandals on their feet but the only way to avoid hypothermia was to keep moving.

The bus driver had disappeared with the keys to the bus. We couldn't open the bus door no matter what we did. The students who were wandering like zombies began to realize that it must be better inside the bus. They began to pound on the door, trying to get in. From inside, we told them, "You have to climb through the window if you want to get in." Many tried and made it, but some of the larger people could not fit through the small window, and were trapped outside. Those who were able to climb into the bus left their tents outside for the stranded ones to wrap themselves in. It was the worst single night I have ever had on an outreach.

When morning came, so did the sickness. Eventually the driver arrived; we all were loaded on the bus and finally set out for the Moldova border. Unfortunately many team members were stricken with diarrhea, and others had a severely painful stomach issue. In contrast, a small number of the team remained free from any type of illness.

It turned out that the non-complainers-club were the only ones who were not stricken with some form of sickness. The delineation between the discontent, grumbling complainers and those of us who had committed to avoid that was really clear. Those who had chosen to complain and grumble had opened themselves to a spiritual attack on their health. Those who had not complained were protected from the attack; same context, same experience, different choices and different outcomes. This lesson was being learned.

Sadly, our situation went from bad to worse. The tour bus had no built-in bathroom, and now many of us were plagued with the need to frequently stop and use the facilities. Finally the bus driver declared through our translator, "Your Romanian visas and travel permits will expire in eight hours; we have to be out of the country in less than eight hours! We cannot stop every five minutes for someone with diarrhea so here is your only option!" To the horror of the sick team members, he was pointing at a five-gallon bucket placed on the lower step of the front entryway to the bus.

No one wanted to choose option A (the bucket). Think about it. But it turned out there was an option B. The team leaders had provided many, many diapers for their children to use during this outreach. It seemed like there were hundreds of diapers stashed in every possible travel bag, and now we had a great need for them. Option B was announced! "If you don't want to use the bucket in the stairwell you can wear Huggies!"

Mortified, the once-proud and complaining group of students now meekly raised their hands to request the diapers in order to avoid the prospect of the white bucket. There was no room left for pride. A meaningful scripture comes to mind whenever I recall this day. The restored Old Testament King, Nebuchadnezzar, said, *"Now I, Nebuchadnezzar, praise, exalt and honor the King of heaven, for all His works are true and His ways just, and He is able to humble those who walk in pride."* (Dan 4:37)

As we hurried along the narrow Romanian highway, racing to get to the border before our papers expired, our small group of non-complainers huddled together in the back of the bus. The lessons of this particular teachable moment were clear to everyone. For eight hours we heard students repeatedly calling out for another diaper. Sadly, as we drove along they had to toss the discarded diapers out the bus window. The absurdity of the situation reduced us to tears of laughter.

Life and outreach will always have their wilderness seasons. The course of your life will be affected by the choices you make when in that wilderness. What should be done when you arrive in the wilderness? Referring back when the ancient Israelites wandered in the wilderness after leaving Egypt, the Apostle Paul gives some strong advice to believers.

> *"Today if you hear His voice, Do not harden your hearts, as when they provoked Me." For who provoked Him when they had heard? Indeed, did not all those who came out of Egypt led by Moses? And with whom was He angry for forty years? Was it not with those who sinned, whose bodies fell in the wilderness?"* (Heb 3:12-17)

When you find yourself in the wilderness it is far too easy to complain and provoke God. Once you have stopped believing that God is good (all the time) and that His intentions and plans for you are good, you defame God. This is exactly what the Israelites did when they accused God in the wilderness.

Deuteronomy 1:27 says, *"and you grumbled in your tents and said, '**Because the LORD hates us**, He has brought us out of the land of Egypt to deliver us into the hand of the Amorites to destroy us.'"*

Did the Lord really hate them? Absolutely not. But their hearts became hardened against God because they chose to believe a lie regarding God's nature and character. They began to define God through the lens of their circumstances rather than to see their circumstances through the eyes of God.

It is a temptation, during an outreach wilderness season, to blame God or attribute evil or suffering to the will of God. Instead, hold on to the truth of who God is, view Him as He says he is and avoid defaming the character of our gracious father in heaven.

James 1:17 says, "*Every good thing given and every perfect gift is from above, coming down from the Father of lights, with whom there is no variation or shifting shadow.*"

It is a tragedy that so many people choose to demean God during seasons of hardship. Sometimes by outright accusations or possibly by attributing evil to Him, "*with whom there is no variation or shifting shadow.*" Either way, your heart can become hardened through unbelief. God wants to see if you will recognize Him and hear His voice even in the midst of the storm. If you do, you will likely find yourself walking on water.

Ask yourself, "How did God view the very same set of wilderness circumstances that the Israelites found themselves in?" (Deut 1:27) Was he an angry God who hated his children and had brought them out to the wilderness to die? This is what the Israelites believed. But from God's perspective the same situations take on an entirely different appearance. Deuteronomy 1:31 says "*... in the wilderness where you saw how* **the LORD your God carried you, just as a man carries his son,** *in all the way which you have walked until you came to this place.*"

The wilderness experience itself is not as it seems. God has the correct perspective on every season in life. No one denies the wilderness was real, or that it was brutal. However, these ferocious circumstances were a perfect storm that allowed God to reveal His true character to His people. God was proving Himself as a loving father who was carrying His children through to the place of rest, the promised land. When you accuse God you may feel like you are walking the wilderness alone. Instead, remember God, remember what he has shown you, and let your loving heavenly father carry you through.

When in an outreach wilderness, or for that matter, any wilderness:

- Avoid grumbling, murmuring or complaining at all costs
- Don't accuse or slander God
- Don't blame God for things that are the fruit of sinful, rebellious humans and fallen angels
- Choose to look for the voice and leading of your heavenly father
- See the storm as an opportunity to walk on water rather than as the wrath of God
- Don't rebel against God or your leadership

- Let God carry you through the wilderness
- Understand that God knows exactly what you are going through and He will deliver you
- Recognize that character is formed in the desert. Wilderness seasons can be exactly what we need
- Remember that God cares for you and is carrying you through to the end
- We learn discipline in the desert so we can reach our destiny

Conclusion

THE FORMAL TRAINING WE ALL EXPERIENCE IN preparing for outreach is valuable. Such training is valuable. But these training components risk being only a theory, until the learning endures real testing. When preparing for outreach, and getting ready to test the theories of discipleship and witness that you have embraced, we each can benefit from hearing about the real world experiences of others. In part, this is there are leaders involved in any effort to advance the Kingdom of God.

The first century Christians also proved in their own experience that *"we must go through many hardships to enter the kingdom of God"*. (Rom 14:22)

In this book we have journeyed together through many real life stories. My goal in sharing these stories was to introduce you to various discipleship topics relevant to an outreach context. I have not intended to compile the exhaustive study of all things related to outreach. It is my desire that you will be equipped to succeed; that you will not be overwhelmed as you step into outreach. Many other theological and missiological books and resources are available to you. Use them. Study them. They will be greatly valuable to you in all aspects of life. Still, these resources might leave you wondering, "How does it work out in real life?"

My goal in recalling these incredible experiences and life lessons is to help you build a strong foundation from which to begin your Kingdom endeavors. Too many people start out from ground level and never have the chance to stand on the shoulders of those who have advanced the Kingdom before them. I desire that my account of the great works of God, achieved through average disciples like me, will give you a chance to go further and accomplish even greater things in the Lord.

My hope is that this book has given you a glimpse into the nature of the battle we all will face as we seek first the kingdom of God. In the war for souls of men there are no easy battles. But nothing else even comes close to the experience of fighting alongside our heavenly Father and seeing the power of God in action.

Your life story is being written. What will your story be? The choices are yours. You may think that you will never write a book or have powerful experiences to share with those who come after you. Remember, God is writing down your story even now.

Live your life in such a way that heaven is enthralled by your exploits and hell wishes you had never been born. If you draw close to the Lord with a heart to understand Him and really know Him, you will begin to value what He values and think about what matters to Him. His victories will become your victories and your victories will matter in eternity. Your outreach matters. You matter.

CPSIA information can be obtained
at www.ICGtesting.com
Printed in the USA
FSOW04n2022221016
26318FS